Encountering Jesus in the Gospels

Books by William C. Mills

Pastoral Ministry

Church, World, and Kingdom: The Eucharistic Foundations of Alexander Schmemann's Pastoral Theology

Kyprian Kern: Orthodox Pastoral Service

Called to Serve: Readings on Ministry From the Orthodox Church

Church and World: Essays in Honor of Michael Plekon

Biblical Prayer and Spirituality

A 30 Day Retreat: A Personal Guide to Spiritual Renewal

Walking with God: Stories of Life and Faith

Come Follow Me

The Prayer of St. Ephrem: A Biblical Commentary

Our Father: A Prayer for Christian Living

Encountering Jesus in the Gospels

Lectionary Series

A Light to the Gentiles: Reflections on the Gospel of Luke

Baptize All Nations: Reflections on the Gospel of Matthew for the Pentecostal Season

Feasts of Faith: Reflections on the Major Feast Days

From Pascha to Pentecost: Reflections on the Gospel of John

Let Us Atend: Reflections on the Gospel of Mark for the Lenten Season

Prepare O Bethlehem: Reflections on the Scripture Readings for the Christmas-Epiphany Season

ENCOUNTERING JESUS IN THE GOSPELS

William C. Mills

First Published by Orthodox Research Institute, 2012
Reprinted by OCABS Press, 2016

© 2012 William C. Mills

Front cover photo credit: Dickran Kouymjian, Index of Armenian Art, Manuscript Illumination, Jerusalem, Armenian Patriarchate, ms J2556, Gospels of King Gagik-Abas of Kars, ca. 1050, fol. 330: Jesus and the rich young man.

ISBN: 1-60191-037-1 (Paperback)

TABLE OF CONTENTS

INTRODUCTION

I have encountered many people who want to learn more about Jesus and who seek an authentic Christian faith but are tired of pleasant platitudes or dry dogmatic formulas that are often heard in Sunday sermons: "If you tithe, God will bless you" or "Just have faith and you will be okay" or even worse, the pastor will provide a long list of do's and don'ts for their congregation, "don't watch TV, don't read the internet" and so forth.

Furthermore, people also encounter fire and brimstone images of Jesus, images that instill unnecessary guilt and shame rather than images of Jesus as a loving, merciful, and compassionate God. No wonder why so many people leave the Church! When people encounter narrow and limited images of Jesus, they leave Church half-empty, seeking more for their spiritual life.

One obvious response is to encourage people to read the entire Bible on their own, especially the New

Testament and particularly the four gospels. The Bible, however, is not the easiest book to read, and people need guidance and instruction. The Bible contains words, images, metaphors, that are often confusing to the modern reader. Furthermore, it seems that every year new books about Jesus are published, many of which are usually too scholarly for the average person who wants to learn about Jesus, but does not want to read an entire Bible commentary.

This book can help. *Encountering Jesus in the Gospels* highlights fifteen Gospel images of Jesus: Jesus the Rabbi, Jesus the Shepherd, Jesus the Lamb, Jesus the Resurrection, and Jesus the Peacemaker, among others. Each particular Gospel image focuses on one essential aspect of Jesus' ministry. Upon finishing this book, you might even find inspiration to read the gospels on your own and begin a more thorough study of the Bible.

MAY THE REAL JESUS PLEASE STAND UP! When you attended Sunday School as a child, you were probably told that there is one Jesus in the gospels. Your teacher was wrong. Wrong you say? Yes, wrong. Well, sort of wrong. According to historical records, there was a person named Jesus of Nazareth who had a band of followers called disciples, you may have learned about them too: Peter, James, John, Judas, Bartholomew, and so forth. You probably know that Jesus was betrayed by Judas, was crucified by the Roman Governor Pontius Pilate, was buried, and was raised from the dead on the third day. However, while there is one Jesus, there are four different accounts or stories about this person Jesus.

We come to know Jesus through four Christian documents that we call the gospels: Matthew, Mark, Luke, and John. The word *gospel* literally means good news, as in the *good news* of Matthew or the *good news* of John. If we read just one of the gospels, we will have a limited and narrow view of Jesus and His ministry. For example, if we only read the Gospel of Mark, we will see that Jesus spends all His time running around Galilee performing a lot of miracles: cleansing lepers, healing the sick, and raising the dead. Mark's gospel, unlike the others, does not contain lengthy sermons or teachings. Mark's gospel is lean and mean. Mark's gospel is also the shortest gospel, it only has sixteen chapters. Matthew's gospel is much longer than Mark and includes the Sermon on the Mount, the Lord's Prayer. Matthew also includes the stories of Jesus' birth as well as His baptism in the Jordan River. When reading the Gospel of Luke, we begin Jesus' story not with Him but with His cousin, John the Baptist. Luke shows his readers the long line of prophetic activity stemming from the Old Testament, through John the Baptist, and then to Jesus. We see Jesus from His infancy until He is about twelve years of age, and then the next time we see Him, He is an adult who begins His preaching and teaching ministry. John's gospel has an altogether different feel than the other gospels. In the Gospel of John, Jesus speaks at length about eternal life and performs many miracles such as changing water into wine and raising Lazarus from the dead.

Parishioners often ask, "Well, which gospel shows us the *true Jesus*?" My answer is always the same, "They all do!"—an answer, of course, which people do not like very much. I then share with them the following example. While on the way home from work you witness a car accident, one car crosses over the yellow line in the middle of the road hits another car. You call 911, and a few minutes later the police show up. Very often the first thing that happens is that the police officer identifies people who saw the car accident so that he can ascertain the facts of the accident. If the police find more than one witness, all the better. However, having more than one witness may not always bring more clarity.

A few years ago while walking past the Lincoln Park Zoo in Chicago, I witnessed a car accident. I was walking down the street towards Lake Michigan and all of a sudden a motorcycle came from my left side and slammed right into the back of an SUV. The driver of the motorcycle fell to his side and rolled a few feet until he stopped in front of me near the sidewalk. Thankfully, no one was hurt. From my perspective, the guy on the motorcycle did not put on his breaks quick enough and was driving faster than he should have been, especially during rush hour. When the guy on the motorcycle got up from the ground, he began yelling at the driver of the SUV for cutting him off and not using his turning signal. While walking down the street, I heard the screeching of tires and the motorcycle hitting the SUV, but I did not see the problem with the turn signal nor did I see that the SUV had stopped. This is precisely the reason why police officers like to have more than one witness. One witness might not even have all the facts either.

We see from this brief example that the gospels do not give us a Polaroid picture of Jesus with specific details about His daily life: what He ate, what He drank, the clothes that He wore, or what He did every single day. When I was a young boy, I always wondered if Jesus liked soccer, which is a logical question for a ten-year-old boy! These particular questions, while they may pique our interest, are not really appropriate because the gospels are not interested in these questions. The gospels are nothing like the biographies of Abraham Lincoln or Eleanor Roosevelt, which present the reader with numerous details regarding personality traits, mannerisms, and daily activities. The four gospels are primarily interested with the good news of the Kingdom of God, a message repeated throughout the gospels and incarnated in Jesus' teaching and preaching.

I guess you can say that the four gospels provide us with a series of impressions of Jesus, like the nineteenth century impressionist paintings by Monet, Renoir, or Cezanne, who painted with broad-brush strokes on large canvases that depicted persons and places in basic shapes and contours, but offer little by ways of precise details. The impressionist painter invites the viewer to connect the dots on his or her own in their minds eye. These very broad impressions make up the complete picture. When looking at the four gospels, we can look at Jesus' many names as broad-brush strokes giving us different images of His life and ministry. When looked at on their own, each impression gives us one aspect of Jesus; however, when taken together in full, they give us a more nuanced and overall picture of Jesus' preaching and teaching ministry.

So What's In A Name Anyway? Every day we encounter different types of names: street names, city names, restaurant names, store names, as well as the various names found in creation, dog, cat, house, truck, trees, plants, animals, stars, and planets. Names are everywhere. When we are introduced to someone new, the first thing we generally say is, "Hello, may name is…, what is your name?" Names are such a big part of our life that we forget how essential they are to our daily life.

The Bible is full of names, many of which are very strange, how many of your friends are named Delilah, Methuselah, or Nebuchadnezzar? Or how about place names such as Gilgal, Phoenicia, Bethsaisda, or try this one — Caesarea Maritima? When was the last time you heard the names Shadrach, Meshach, or Abednego? Probably not recently!

Even if someone has never read the Bible, they most likely have heard of the name Jesus. He is very popular in our modern culture. At least once a day I see either a billboard sign or bumper sticker with the name Jesus on it. The average Joe or Jane Doe may even know a little something about Jesus' life and ministry: that He was born in Bethlehem, lived in Nazareth, had a band of twelve men called disciples, performed miracles, was crucified, and rose on the third day. If you ask them anything else, their faces go a blank because that is where their knowledge ends. I used to begin classes on the New Testament with a quiz about Jesus, and even some of my *devout* Bible reading students failed.

Did you know that the New Testament contains over seventy-five different images or names of Jesus: Jesus of Nazareth, Son of God, Son of Man, Christ, the Lamb of God, the Bread of Life, Emmanuel, as well as the Alpha and Omega? That is a lot of names! As you can see, the Gospel's authors used common everyday images, like light, bread, shepherd, prophet, to explain Jesus to the people.

Names have always been important. During the Middle Ages, most people lived in small hamlets or villages that were scattered across the countryside. People performed different types of work from baking to glass blowing, some were farmers and day laborers, and others were soldiers and craftsman. In the ancient world, people were identified by their work or vocation: Mary the Baker, Tom the Miller, or Bill the Farmer. Over time, these names were eventually shortened: Mary Baker, Tom Miller, and Bill Farmer. I always wondered if my Danish ancestors had windmills on their property, hence my last name Mills.

While everyone has first and last names like John Smith or Jane Doe, we also have other names that reveal our role or place society. These additional names or titles provide a broader perspective on life. Below is a list of additional names or titles:

Priest
Husband
Dad
Cook
Gardener
Author
Friend
Neighbor

When introducing myself, I usually say, "Hello, my name is Bill." This short introduction gives you a very limited idea of who I am. However, if I say, "Hello, my name is Bill and I am a pastor," you now know that I lead a Christian congregation, but your image of me is still rather limited. If I say, "My name is Father Bill," you will know that I am a priest; however, you need additional information to learn which Church I serve.

Furthermore, through our conversation, you may find out that I love cooking and gardening. Therefore, your mental image of me will broaden: Bill the priest who is also a cook and gardener. In other words, the more information you have about me, the better you will begin to know about my life and my interests. This same principle applies to Jesus. It is one thing to read about Jesus of Nazareth who lived in Galilee and performed miracles, but then it is something different to find out what it meant that he was a Rabbi and that He called Himself a Shepherd and the Bread of Life.

Hopefully, after reading this book, you will have a much broader and nuanced vision of Jesus of Nazareth and His universal call for love, mercy, compassion, and forgiveness. You will learn about a Jesus who cannot be pigeon-holed into a box. As you begin reading, you will find yourself on a life-long spiritual journey.

I encourage you to read this book slowly. Read a chapter one time in order to get a basic understanding and then read it again more slowly. Take time to look up the additional scriptural references in the chapter, since they will add to your understanding. You might want to ask yourself, "What does this particular image of Jesus say to me?" or "How does this particular aspect of Jesus' life affect me?" Each chapter also includes several *Food for Thought* questions, which will also add to your reading. The *Food for Thought* questions will also help with small group discussions, especially if you are using the book for group Bible study or for your spiritual journaling.

CHAPTER ONE

JESUS THE BREAD

"I am the bread of life. Your ancestors ate the manna in the wilderness, and they died. This is the bread that comes down from heaven, so that one may eat of it and not die. I am the living bread that came down from heaven. Whoever eats of this bread will live for ever; and the bread that I will give for the life of the world is My flesh" (John 6:48-51).

I love baking. When I am not at the computer or in the backyard tending my garden or out taking a long walk at the park, you will find me in the kitchen. When we built our new house, we requested that our kitchen have two ovens for my gastronomic creations: pizza, meatloaf, roasts, bread, cakes, and pastries. I enjoy a variety of activities, but baking is my favorite. There is nothing better than squishing your fingers in flour, water, and yeast mixture, making a big mess in the kitchen.

Bread is one of the basic staples of life, and most people eat it at least once a day: toast in the morning, a sandwich for lunch, or a buttered roll or biscuit with dinner. Bread is also known throughout the world; in Spanish-speaking countries, it is called *pan*, in India it is called *chapatti* or *naan*, and in Greece and Lebanon its *pita*.

Three years ago, I went on a ten day Holy Land pilgrimage. One day while walking in Old Jerusalem, I spotted an elderly man pushing a silver cart. Stacked on top of the cart were mounds of freshly baked rectangular sized pita breads stacked at least three feet high. Within minutes, a small crowd formed around the man and his cart. Everyone wanted a loaf of his fresh bread. The man stayed there until all the bread was sold and then wheeled the cart away. His work was done for the day. Every day the man wheeled his cart into the street and every day people bought his bread.

Bread is also mentioned in the Bible. In Exodus, God instructs Moses to leave Egypt because Moses is going to lead the Israelites from slavery to freedom. God's message came so quickly that the Israelites did not have time to pack; they took their belongings and followed Moses across the Red Sea. However, there was a problem. The Israelites left Egypt so quickly that they did not have any food. What were they going to do?

God always had a plan. God told Moses that He was going to send them bread from heaven, which

He called manna. The Bible says that manna looked like white frost on the ground or little puffballs of cotton or white flakes. God commanded the Israelites to gather the manna every day, and gather double portion on Friday since the next day was the Sabbath day, a day of rest. The Israelites must not have liked the manna very much, because they complained to God. They certainly must have eaten a lot of bread during all those years in the wilderness.

Throughout His ministry, Jesus performed many miracles: cleansed the lepers, changed water into wine, cured the blind, and raised the dead. Perhaps one of His most famous miracles is the multiplication of loaves.

While each gospel retells the story a bit differently, John tells us that Jesus went up to a high mountain. There were crowds of people, mostly peasants and farmers, who followed Him all day. It was late in the day, and Jesus looked out and saw the great crowds of hungry poor peasants waiting to eat. His disciples were there, and since they too were tired, they asked Jesus to send the crowds away so that they could rest. The disciples did not want a couple thousand people hanging around at dinnertime! Yet, Jesus refused their request. He fed the people:

> *After this Jesus went to the other side of the Sea of Galilee, also called the Sea of Tiberias. A large crowd kept following him, because they*

saw the signs that he was doing for the sick. Jesus went up the mountain and sat down there with his disciples. Now the Passover, the festival of the Jews, was near. When he looked up and saw a large crowd coming towards him, Jesus said to Philip, 'Where are we to buy bread for these people to eat?' He said this to test him, for he himself knew what he was going to do. Philip answered him, 'Six months' wages would not buy enough bread for each of them to get a little.' One of his disciples, Andrew, Simon Peter's brother, said to him, 'There is a boy here who has five barley loaves and two fish. But what are they among so many people?' Jesus said, 'Make the people sit down.' Now there was a great deal of grass in the place; so they sat down, about five thousand in all. Then Jesus took the loaves, and when he had given thanks, he distributed them to those who were seated; so also the fish, as much as they wanted. When they were satisfied, he told his disciples, 'Gather up the fragments left over, so that nothing may be lost.' So they gathered them up, and from the fragments of the five barley loaves, left by those who had eaten, they filled twelve baskets. When the people saw the sign that he had done, they began to say, 'This is indeed the prophet who is to come into the world' (John 6:1–14).

Jesus ordered His disciples to have the crowds sit down. Jesus then took five loaves of bread and two fish and looked up to heaven, blessed them, broke them, and then gave them to the crowds. John tells us that five thousand people were fed that day, and Matthew tells us that not only was it five thousand men but women and children also. This same story is retold in the other gospels as well (Mt. 14:13–21; Mk. 6:32–44; Lk. 9:10–17).

The gospels portray Jesus as the great provider. In the beginning of John's gospel, Jesus attends a wedding. The wine ran out and his mother asks the servant to bring several jars of water. Jesus then obliges His mother and changes the water into wine, providing enough wine for the crowd. Jesus fed five thousand and seven thousand people with a few loaves of bread and fish. Just before his death, Jesus ate His last Passover meal with His disciples in the Upper Room in Jerusalem. During the meal, Jesus took bread and said, "Take, eat, this is My body which is broken for you," and then a cup of wine and said, "Drink of it all of you, this is My blood." Jesus' last command to His disciples was to break bread with one another, to share a meal. Every time they shared this meal, they were supposed to remember Jesus and His mission. Many Christians throughout the world still celebrate this special meal, which is called the Eucharist or the Lord's Supper, a special meal of bread and wine to remember Jesus and His life-giving words. Roman

Catholics refer to this meal as the Mass, and Eastern Christians, namely Byzantine Catholics and Eastern Orthodox, call it the Divine Liturgy.

Every Sunday, we gather together and celebrate the same meal that Jesus served for His disciples. However, we often forget that Jesus comes to us in the *broken bread* as we hear in the gospels, "Take, eat, this is My body which is *broken for you*." Jesus comes to us in His frailty and brokenness. I always found this hard to believe that the same person who walked on water, who raised the dead, who cured lepers, comes to us every week in His brokenness. As a psychologist friend once told me, pain speaks to pain, or suffering speaks to suffering. The word *sympathy* means to feel pain with someone else, to identify your pain with someone else's pain. Every Sunday Jesus identifies with us in *our* fallen humanity, *our* sinfulness, and *our* brokenness. In turn, Jesus asks us to do the same with the rest of the world. In the multiplication of loaves, Jesus does not feed the crowd Himself, He tells His disciples, *"You give them something to eat"* or in other words, you feed them.

Many people take this feeding image to heart. Sara Miles, journalist and author of the book *Take This Bread* and more recently her new book *Jesus Freak*, is an adult convert to Christianity. In her two books, Miles describes her newly found ministry as coordinator of her parish food program. Through Sara's reading of the gospels and living and praying with the Christian community at St. Gregory of Nyssa Episcopal Church in San Francisco, CA, Sara realized that Jesus was dead serious about feeding people and that, at the feast of Pentecost, the Holy Spirit was given to the disciples not to remain in Jerusalem, but to go out and preach, heal, and feed.

After months of planning and organizing, Sara convinced her parish that they needed to start a food pantry ministry out of their Church. St. Gregory's is located in a very transient neighborhood, which includes many homeless, poor, and hungry people. A small idea blossomed. Today, hundreds of homeless people, black, white, brown, men and women, young and old, come for a hot lunch and share hospitality and fellowship with the members of St. Gregory's. Not only do these people receive a hot meal, but they are also encouraged to take a bag of fresh fruit and vegetables with them when they leave.

Most food banks are located in multi-purpose buildings or in Church basements, but not at St. Gregory's! Sara made sure that her food bank was located right in the middle of the Church building, where every Sunday her fellow parishioners hear the Gospel and break bread. Once a week tables and chairs are set up around the altar, and people come and eat, re-creating in a way Jesus' multiplication of loaves miracle. Sara and her fellow parishioners are convinced that Jesus is the Bread of Life and share their own bread with their neighbors and friends.

Sara, of course, is not alone. She stands in a long line of other men and women devoted to caring for the poor and hungry, both in very physical and more often in spiritual ways. Dorothy Day, the editor of the *Catholic Daily Worker*, a nationwide newspaper, and social organizer, established houses of hospitality around the slums of New York City. Every day workers at these houses served thousands of indigent men and women, many of whom were alcoholics, drug users, and prostitutes. Dorothy did not care. She was following Jesus' command to feed Jesus' little flock. The Orthodox nun and writer Mother Maria Skobtsova did the same thing as Dorothy. During World War II, Mother Maria searched and scoured the dumpsters and garbage cans of Paris searching for scraps of food, which she brought home to her small community on Rue Lourmel so she could make soup and feed the hungry men, women, and children. There are hundreds of people like Sara, Dorothy, and Mother Maria, who fed and continue to feed the hungry and homeless.

Many people are also familiar with the work and ministry of Mother Teresa of Calcutta who not only took care of lepers and infants, but she fed lots of people not only with her spiritual wisdom and teachings but also with food. The poor and hungry would line up every day outside her spiritual houses in order to receive some bread, rice, and fresh water. One could also include other noteworthy persons of faith, such as the late Catholic priest and spiritual author Henri Nouwen, who devoted his life to caring for the mentally ill at the L'Arche center in Canada, or the Orthodox monk and hermit, Herman of Alaska, who lived a simple life on Kodiak Island, where he helped the poor, orphan, and abused.

By feeding and serving other people, whether it is a hot cup of coffee and a bagel, or through feeding them with a kind word or a hug, we are following Jesus' command to love our neighbors. Often we forget that the small things in life are the ones that matter the most. There were times in parish ministry when I was down and out and one of my friends called me every day just to make sure that I was okay. He was feeding me with his kind words. Every day I am fed and nourished in so many ways, a continuation of Jesus' ministry as the Bread of Life, offering Himself as food for His followers. The least we can do is share some of our bread with those people around us, a way to continue Jesus' feeding ministry.

FOOD FOR THOUGHT

1. Take some time to reflect on Jesus as the Bread of Life. How is Jesus bread for you? How does He nourish and feed you?

2. When Jesus multiplied the loaves and fish, the Gospel of John says that there were twelve baskets full of food left over. Jesus provides an abundant feast. How can you share your abundance with others? How can you share your life with those who are in need? What prevents you from sharing your life with others?

3. Take time and think about the people or organizations that have fed and nourished you during your lifetime. Offer a prayer of thanksgiving for these people as they continue to feed and nourish the world.

4. For further reading: John 6, Matthew 20, and Mark 15, Luke 24, John 21.

CHAPTER TWO

JESUS THE SHEPHERD

'I am the good shepherd. The good shepherd lays down his life for the sheep. The hired hand, who is not the shepherd and does not own the sheep, sees the wolf coming and leaves the sheep and runs away — and the wolf snatches them and scatters them. The hired hand runs away because a hired hand does not care for the sheep. I am the good shepherd. I know My own and My own know me, just as the Father knows Me and I know the Father. And I lay down My life for the sheep. I have other sheep that do not belong to this fold. I must bring them also, and they will listen to My voice. So there will be one flock, one shepherd (John 10:11–16).

Most of us live in either suburban or urban areas. We usually see more roads and sidewalks than we do grass, fields, and farms. Most of us do not see sheep wandering around our neighborhoods ei-

ther. I live in the suburbs, and once in a while, I will
see an occasional wild turkey or deer jumping across
the road or a horse or two grazing in the nearby farm
fields, but I do not see much livestock, at least not in
my neck of the woods. If you wake up in the morning
and find a few sheep in your backyard, you better call
animal control!

Several years ago, our family took a two-week
trip to Scotland, a country with more sheep than
people. When driving up and down the mountains
and through the valleys and across the rivers, we saw
thousands of sheep. Sheep were everywhere: on the
side of the road, high up on the mountaintop, and
down in the valleys. Of course, lamb was also on the
dinner menu. Every pub and restaurant served some
variety of lamb: rack of lamb, lamb burgers, lamb
roasts, leg of lamb — all, of course, served with the
prerequisite side order of boiled potatoes and peas,
which was is washed down with a pint of ale.

Unlike most of us today, Jesus lived in an agrar-
ian culture. I met a few people who grew up on farms,
but they are really few and far between. During Jesus'
time, the majority of people were farmers who raised
wheat, figs, grapes, and legumes. Others were peasants and day-laborers working on large farms; others
were bakers, leather workers, blacksmiths, potters,
carpenters, stonemasons and shepherds, not to men-
tion, of course, fishermen and other various types of
tradesmen such as glass blowers or cobblers.

Sheep were an essential part of the economy; they were raised for both their wool and their meat. Every year at Passover, the Jews were commanded to offer a young lamb as a thanksgiving offering to God. Other Jewish festivals also required sheep as well. The Temple priests slaughtered the lambs, drained the blood, and cooked the meat. As payment, the priests took a portion of the meat for themselves and then gave the remaining portion back to the person who offered the meat. You can imagine the stench in ancient Jerusalem, smoke rising from the fire pits, as the Temple priests roasted the lambs. Even today, while strolling through the narrow alleys of the Old City in Jerusalem, you will see sheep carcasses hanging in the butcher shop. If you are lucky, you might see an old man with a freshly butchered lamb over his shoulder, which he will most likely bring home to cook on an open fire pit, with rosemary and garlic, and served with fresh rice and pita bread, a Mediterranean delicacy.

In the Gospel of John, Jesus refers to Himself as the good shepherd, "I am the good shepherd, I know the sheep and they sheep know Me. The good shepherd lays down his life for the sheep. He who is a hireling and not a shepherd, whose own the sheep are not, sees the wolf coming and leaves the sheep and flees, and the wolf snatches them and scatters them. He flees because he is a hireling and cares nothing for the sheep" (John 10:11–13). However, Jesus is not the only shepherd mentioned in the Scriptures. Jesus actually comes from a long line of shepherds going all the way back to the Old Testament. Jacob, Moses, Joseph, David were all shepherds. They tended their flocks and cared for their sheep. God the Father is sometimes referred to as a shepherd watching over and caring for Israel. In the following passage, the Patriarch Jacob, in his old age, blesses his son Joseph before he dies, "The God before whom my ancestors Abraham and Isaac walked, *the God who has been my shepherd* all my life to this day" (Gen. 48:15). Jacob refers to God as his shepherd, guiding him and leading him to life, a theme that we see throughout the Old and New Testaments.

When thinking of shepherds, we conjure up Hollywood images of cowboys, like Roy Rogers or John Wayne or Big John from Bonanza—rough and tough guys riding fast horses and using cattle prods making sure the cattle were all headed in the right direction. However, in the Middle East, things work differently. Sheep are very dumb animals. If left to their own, they would walk off a cliff if they knew there was food down in the valley. Therefore, the shepherd must take very good care to know his sheep; he cannot let them get lost or harmed. Usually, the shepherd walks ahead of the sheep rather than from behind making sounds with his mouth or with a little bell or metal rattle so the sheep will know where the shepherd is headed. The shepherd walks in front of the large flock of sheep leading them to safety for the night or to streams of water for drink or to green pastures for food. The shepherds know the lay of the land; the mountains and valleys, the streams and rivers. Shepherds need to know where they are going; otherwise, they will get lost and so will the sheep. A wise shepherd knows the terrain and his sheep well; otherwise, he will be in big trouble.

One day as our pilgrimage group was taking a bus trip towards the Dead Sea in the southern part of Israel not too far from the Negev desert, I looked outside my window and saw a Palestinian Bedouin shepherd with dark tan wrinkly skin with a brass bell in one hand, and a walking stick in the other with fifteen little sheep behind him. The man looked like a schoolteacher followed by fifteen little children. Since it was very hot and dry, the shepherd was looking for a small stream so that his sheep could drink some water. The shepherd looked tired as he was leading those sheep all day through the hot June sun. His job was to take care of those sheep and make sure they had food, water, and shelter.

Shepherds have a difficult job. Sheep need constant care and attention, including eating a lot of food and drinking plenty of water. Furthermore, sheep have to be shorn on a regular basis so that their coats do not get too thick. The shearing process is a tedious one, and it takes a lot of manual labor as well as patience. The shorn wool then has to be sent to local mills for processing, where it is turned into scarves, hats, sweaters, blankets, and other textile products. Shepherding is not a high paying job, so very often shepherds have to supplement their jobs with farming or some other line of work.

When thinking about this Palestinian shepherd and the image of Jesus being the good shepherd, I could not help but think of Psalm 23, a Psalm that is often found on Hallmark cards and prayed at funerals or memorial services. Psalm 23 is a Psalm about God being our shepherd:

> *The Lord is my shepherd I shall not want;*
> *He makes me lie down in green pastures.*
> *He leads me beside still waters;*
> *He restores my soul*
> *He leads me in right paths for his name's sake*
> *Even though I walk through the darkest valley,*
> *I fear no evil;*
> *For you are with me;*
> *Your rod and your staff,*
> *They comfort me.*
> *You prepare a table before me in the presence of my enemies;*
> *You anoint my head with oil;*
> *My cup overflows.*
> *Surely goodness and mercy shall follow me*
> *All the days of my life,*
> *And I shall dwell in the house of the Lord my whole life long.*

When reading slowly, take in every word as it comes to you. Read the first verse, "The Lord is my shepherd." What does it mean that the Lord is described as a shepherd? How is the Lord your shepherd? If the Lord is described as a shepherd, this means that we are His sheep. How are we like sheep? Do we always follow Him where He leads us? Are we always obedient to His every command? Very often I act just like one of those stubborn sheep that tries to leave the flock and do my own thing! Yet Jesus wants me back in His flock; He wants me to come and follow. He wants me to listen to Him and to follow Him. Even though we are not always cute and cuddly like the sheep in the nursery rhymes, He nonetheless cares for each and every one of His little lambs. What a beautiful image to have of Jesus, as a gentle shepherd ready to provide care and consolation to us no matter how strong headed, stubborn, and unlovable as we may be, He always is there showing us the way.

FOOD FOR THOUGHT

1. Sheep are stubborn and often go with the whims of the flock. Wherever one sheep goes, the others follow. Do you find yourself going your own way not trying to follow the still small voice of God?

2. How can you be a better disciple? Think of practical ways that Jesus can be the center of your life.

3. Sheep tend to travel in herds or packs, they stay together in community. How can you help other sheep in your local parish community follow Jesus so that you will stay together? What are some things that you can do to make your community strong?

4. For further reading: Ezekiel 34, Psalm 23, John 10.

CHAPTER THREE

JESUS THE KING

"Your Kingdom come, Your will be done on earth as it is in heaven" (Matt. 6:10).

A while back, I had trouble sleeping, so I walked downstairs and turned on the television. To my surprise, the royal wedding was being broadcast live from London: Prince William and Catherine Middleton were getting married. I did not plan to watch the wedding but since I was already awake and there was nothing else was on at 5:30 AM, I decided to stay up and watch. The wedding was like a fairy tale. Kate arrived at Westminster Cathedral in a shiny black limousine. She wore a long white dress with a short train, a diamond crown on her head, and a sheer veil covering her face. Prince William was decked out in his military finest: red jacket, gold sash and dark pants. He looked stunning. The guest list included government officials, heads of state, ambassadors from around the world, important dignitaries, pop star idols, as well as friends and family members. Two choirs sang the responses. The entire wedding service was fit for a king. Afterwards Kate and William, now referred to as the Duke and Duchess of Cambridge, left the cathedral in a red horse drawn carriage. They arrived at Buckingham Palace in central London for their reception and party.

Jesus began His life as a king, albeit a baby king. At the beginning of Matthew's gospel, wise men traveled to Bethlehem because they noticed the star in the East. However, before visiting the baby Jesus, they first visited with King Herod, announcing to him the good news, "Where is the child who has been born king of the Jews? For we observed His star at its rising, and we have come to pay Him homage" (Matt. 2:1–2). This news sends Herod into a wild rage, and he orders all two-year-old boys and younger to be killed. Eventually, the Magi find the Christ child and brought Him gifts of gold, frankincense, and myrrh.

Jesus was born in a kingdom called the Roman Empire. The Roman Empire stretched all the way from Northern England, through most of central Europe, and also North Africa. The Roman Emperor was in charge of the military and armed forces. The emperor collected taxes, made laws, and built roads and bridges. The Gospel of Luke mentions that Jesus was born under the reign of Augustus, "In those days a decree went out from Emperor Augustus that all the world should be registered" (Luke 2:1). Augustus was one of the most important rulers of the Roman Empire. He was the adopted son of the famous Emperor Julius Caesar. Augustus was considered a good emperor, and it was during his reign that many famous Roman construction projects were erected.

Jesus was also born during the reign of the Jewish rulers called the Herodians. The Herodians were a very wealthy Jewish aristocratic family that ruled most of Palestine. King Herod put John the Baptist to death, and then later, he put Jesus to death. Herod was very powerful, and during the reign of Herod, the Great the Temple in Jerusalem was constructed. Even though the Romans ruled over the land, they allowed the Jews to rule the people in Judea (modern-day Israel) since the Jews had their own religious rules and regulations as well. Essentially the people lived under two forms of government, the Roman Empire and the local Jewish kings.

When Jesus began preaching the Gospel, He said, "Behold the *Kingdom of God* is at hand." We may read or hear about the Kingdom of God, but we usually do not give it a second thought. The gospels speak very much about the Kingdom of Heaven or the Kingdom of God. When we hear that Jesus lived under the reign of two very important and powerful people, Augustus and King Herod, we realize the impact of Jesus' preaching. Jesus came not just to start a religious or political rebellion, but to herald in God's reign, God's Kingdom.

When people heard Jesus talk about the Kingdom of Heaven or the Kingdom of God, they probably looked around and thought that Jesus was planning to build an earthly kingdom, after all, they interacted with the Roman Empire on a daily basis. They visited Roman temples and markets, traveled across Roman engineered bridges, encountered Roman soldiers, used Roman money, paid their Roman taxes, used roads and seaports built by Roman slaves and workers, and lived under laws created by the Roman government. Everyday people encountered various parts of the Roman Empire.

When reading the Gospel, we know that Jesus was not interested in creating yet another earthly empire like the Egyptians, Assyrians, Hittites, or Phoenicians. Jesus was not interested in buildings, temples, land, money, treasure, and power. He was not interested in conquest and building new earthly cities and towns. Jesus taught His followers that He was anointed to bring God's Kingdom, which was not of this world. Jesus did not set out to overthrow the Roman or Jewish government but to show people that there was an alternative way to live.

People had a difficult time understanding what Jesus meant. After all the phrase, *Kingdom of God* sounds abstract. When people heard the word *kingdom*, they would have immediately thought about the Roman Empire. They saw signs and symbols of either the Roman government or the Jewish rulers. Every day people used coins stamped with the face of either the Herodian Kings or the Roman Emperor. Roman soldiers could be found in every seaport and city, goods and services were heavily taxed by both the Romans and the Jewish leaders. Water was brought to villages, towns, and cities by Roman engineered aqueduct systems that crisscrossed the land. The Romans constructed well-built roads that connected cites across the empire. Roman roads that were built during the time of Jesus are still around today. All of this was done under the Roman emperors and for the glory of Rome. Yet Jesus still preached the Kingdom of God had come.

Jesus told His followers that His Father's Kingdom was not like the Roman or Jewish kingdoms. Jesus said that His Father's kingdom was not of this world. In order to explain Himself, Jesus used very practical everyday images:

> *"The kingdom of heaven is like a mustard seed that someone took and sowed in his field; it is the smallest of all the seeds, but when it has grown it is the greatest of shrubs and becomes a tree, so that the birds of the air come and make nests in its branches" (Matt. 13:31–32).*

> *"The kingdom of heaven is like yeast that a woman took and mixed in with three measures of flour until all of it was leavened" (Matt. 13:33).*

"Again the kingdom of heaven is like a merchant in search of fine pearls; on finding one pearl of great value, he went and sold all that he had and bought it" (Matt. 13:45).

"Again, the kingdom of heaven is like a net that was thrown into the sea and caught fish of every kind; when it was full, they drew it ashore, sat down and put the good into baskets but threw out the bad" (Matt. 13:47-48).

Jesus was a great teacher. He knew that His audience was primarily poor illiterate peasant farmers and laborers. However, Jesus got His point across by using everyday images such as mustard plants, pearls, and yeast. Jesus expected that when proclaimed, the Gospel of the Kingdom, people would understand what he was talking about. People knew what mustard plants were and about yeast and flour.

Jesus also taught His disciples and followers that His kingdom was not like the kingdom of the Roman Emperors or the Jewish leaders. His Father's kingdom was about conquering new lands or building roads, buildings, and bridges. No. Jesus' message was about conquering the world with love, peace, unity, justice forgiveness, mercy, patience, and truth. The slaves and servants were not to serve only the rich and the wealthy but to serve one another. He told them that the last shall be first and the first shall be last. He told them that, in this world, the poor and homeless are oppressed and the wealthier and powerful rule. However, in the Kingdom of God, there will be a big role reversal, those who are sinners, prostitutes, beggars, and homeless will enter before the wealthy and powerful. God's kingdom is not of this world.

Jesus also told His followers that not only did He come to bring the kingdom, but that each of us has a very important role to play. There is no such thing as a passive Christian. The Apostle Paul says that in our baptism, we have been given new life, "Therefore, we have been buried with Him by baptism into death, so that, just as Christ was raised from the dead by the glory of the Father, so we too might walk in newness of life" (Romans 6). New life! Now that sounds wonderful. But we need to remember that this new life is a gift from God and that we need not only to cherish it, but also to live each day sharing the love, peace, and joy of the kingdom with the people around us.

When reading the gospels, you may not think of Jesus as a king since He lived a life of complete poverty. He did not live in a large royal palace nor did He travel with a large retinue of soldiers and royal officials. You will not find coins minted with His face on it, nor will you see large temples and buildings dedicated in His honor. Jesus did not own any property and never used His power to hurt anyone. He did not go to war. Jesus was a humble and lowly king, a servant of servants. He taught His followers about caring for one another and following Him to the ends of the earth preaching and teaching the Gospel. He did not promise them power and glory, but rather He warned them that they might be detained, arrested, or even put to death. He told them that people might not want to hear the message, and if they do not, well, no sweat, just keep on moving on! Towards the end of His life, He entered Jerusalem in royal fashion; however, he did not do it in a golden horse drawn carriage but on a donkey (John 12:12–20).

When asked how a Christian should live in our world, I always tell them that we live according to the kingdom. We live as if we were already in the kingdom of God! Now this may seem overwhelming, but really it is not. Every single day we have many opportunities to practice our Christian faith in small ways by being kind to strangers and neighbors, sharing our worldly possessions with those who are in need of them. We can forgive others and show little and big acts of love. Every day there are dozens of opportunities where we can live according to the Kingdom of God. We need to remember though that we also have to abide by the rules of this world, which means following the rules of our government and paying our taxes, even Jesus told us to render to Caesar what is Caesar's, and to God that which is from God! Yet, our main objective is to live according to the Kingdom of God and follow Jesus the best we can each and every day.

Food For Thought

1. Jesus says that His Father's Kingdom is not of this world. Do you live according to this Kingdom? Do you practice love, mercy, peace, justice, and forgiveness? If not, what prevents you from practicing these basic Christian virtues?

2. In the Lord's Prayer we pray, "Thy kingdom come, Thy will be done." Very often we put our will first before God. Do you believe these words?

3. For further reading: Matthew 5–7, 1 Corinthians 12, Romans 6, Ephesians 4.

CHAPTER FOUR

JESUS THE PEACEMAKER

"Blessed are the peacemakers, for they will be called children of God" (Matt. 5:9).

We live in a time of war and conflict. Every time I turn on the television, there is yet another war breaking out somewhere in the world: Iraq, Afghanistan, Libya, Sudan, Yemen, and Ethiopia. Major revolutions are taking place in Syria, Egypt, Tunisia, and across the Arab world. Almost every continent has some war or civil unrest. Sometimes it may be a war fought with weapons, and other times it could be a war fought with words and ideas: Christians versus Muslims, Jews versus Christians, Democrats versus Republicans, whites versus blacks, rich versus poor, conservative versus liberal. Every generation has their own wars, divisions, and disagreements.

Wars can be fought on large scales, as we see in Iraq or Afghanistan, and also on small scales too. There are wars between families and among individuals. Like most families, my parents fought from time to time. Thankfully, these were not full out battles, more like skirmishes I guess. Sometimes friends get into fights as well. In school, I had fights with friends, mostly who got the best grades or which team was the best in sports. The fourth century pastor and theologian Saint John Chrysostom said that the real battle between good and evil is fought not in some faraway countryside, but the real battle between good and evil, truth and lies, is fought within one's own very heart.

One of Jesus' names is the Prince of Peace. Ironically, Jesus was born during the time of great peace in the Roman Empire, which was called the *Pax Romana* or Roman Peace. For the first time in a long time, the Empire was not fighting a large-scale war. When Augustus became Caesar, one of his promises was to end the bloody battles that cost the Romans both men and money. Yet when the prophet Isaiah spoke about the coming Messiah, he referred to him as the prince of peace. This peace was not like the peace of the Romans. The problem with this type of peace is that eventually this peace breaks down. Husbands and wives may love each other and have long times of peace, but once in a while, a skirmish or two starts up and then you have World War III on your hands. The same pertains to governments, at one time country A and country B coexist peacefully and then the next time they are fighting one another.

It seems like humans just cannot live together peacefully, we always have to argue about something.

The Hebrew word for peace is *shalom*. Shalom means unity and wholeness, completeness and goodness. When we are at peace with our enemies, it means that we can live in harmony and oneness not causing strife. Jesus came to bring the peace of God with Him. The word peace occurs many times in the Bible. On Sunday mornings, many pastors begin the worship service with a blessing of peace just as Jesus did when He visited with His disciples on the first Easter Sunday, "Peace be with you" (John 20:19). I know one pastor who every time he greets someone, he says *peace brother* or *peace sister*. I guess he wants to remind people that we are all called to be peacemakers, something about which we need constant reminding.

Even though the Romans had a relatively peaceful time during the first century, there still were many divisions and disagreements among people. Jews did not get along well with their Samaritan neighbors, and Jews and Gentiles did not like one another very much either. Slaves and freemen were at odds with one another, and since women did not have the same rights as men did, they too were separated in community life. No wonder why St. Paul said that there is neither Jew nor Greek, slave or free, or male or female, but Christ is all and in all. In other words, let's stop bickering folks and start loving one another! This is easier said than done. It seems like we would rather argue and bicker than get along with one another.

Jesus was a radical peacemaker. Several times the gospels report that Jesus' disciples wanted to defend Him from the Roman authorities. At one point, when Jesus and His disciples were in the Garden of Gethsemane, Peter took out his sword. Jesus told Peter to put his sword away, those who live by the sword die by the sword. Never once in His life did Jesus fight evil with evil. Jesus always took the upper road, the road less traveled as they say. It is easy to stoop down to darkness and anger, but it is must harder to live with truth, justice, and honesty.

When looking at people in history, I am always amazed with the life and work of Mahatma Gandhi. Gandhi lived during a time of great division in India, and his life and legacy proved him to be a radical peacemaker. The British controlled India. Some political factions in India wanted an armed rebellion to push out the British colonists. Yet, Gandhi had another way, which he called peaceful resistance. Rather than take up arms and fight the British with swords, guns, and power, they would fight the British on peaceful terms, sit-ins, strikes, and shopping at Indian controlled stores rather than British stores. Gandhi forbade any armed rebellion, not even for purposes of defense. Many Indians balked at Gandhi thinking him a fool. Yet, at the end of the day, his way proved right. Over time, the British realized that they could not stop long-term countrywide strikes and sit-ins and marches so they gave up their control of government and left. It is no wonder then why the American Civil Rights movement, started by Martin Luther King Jr. and others, was so successful. Martin Luther King was a student of Gandhi's radical teaching.

Being a peacemaker is not easy. No one said it would be. Yet, Jesus shows us the way. We must first begin with ourselves. We cannot create a peaceful world around us if we ourselves are not at peace. Recently, I have found that keeping a regular spiritual journal to be very helpful. I find that when I get out my problems and issues on paper I feel less hostile during the day. I am more kind and friendly. Of course, this does not always happen but I noticed that when I write down everything that is bothering me, it gets *out of my system* so to speak and, therefore, I do not keep these feelings to myself. Usually, the more that I keep my feelings to myself, the angrier I get and then this anger has to come out somewhere. Usually, it comes out in bad language or a snarky attitude! I also strive to turn the other cheek when I encounter someone with whom I do not agree; I take the upper road and try to be as charitable as I can. Every day we encounter all types of people whom we may not like or get along with, yet we strive to be peacemakers whenever and wherever possible.

Food for Thought

1. Make a list of people whom you have hurt with your words or actions. Pray for them. Pray that you and your friend can be reconciled.

2. Take a few moments and acknowledge the people around you who are peacemakers. Who are they your role models for peace keeping? Make a list of some of their qualities that express a peaceful attitude and try to incarnate those qualities in your life.

3. Strive to be a peacemaker in your life.

4. For further reading: John 20:19–23, Romans 1:1–6, Galatians 1:1–4.

CHAPTER FIVE

JESUS THE PROPHET

When the chief priests and the Pharisees heard His parables, they realized that He was speaking about them. They wanted to arrest Him, but they feared the crowds, because they regarded Him as a prophet (Matt. 21:45-46).

When we hear the word *prophet*, we may think of an odd-looking shabbily dressed guy foretelling the end of the world or someone standing on a street corner yelling and screaming "the end is coming the end is coming." In elementary school, I had a fascination with the infamous prophet Nostradamus. Nostradamus lived in 16th-century Italy. I first heard of him while watching a history program on television and then went straight to the town library and checked out a few books about his life. I was intrigued. Nostradamus predicted the end of the world, the onset of wars and plagues, and coming natural disasters.

Every generation has their own version of Nostradamus. Earlier this year, I was watching the evening news and a pastor in the Southeast United States predicted that, in June 2011, the world was going to end. His parishioners marched on street corners carrying signs warning people that the end of the world was coming soon. The media had a field day, especially when the appointed "end of the world" day in June never took place. Life went on as usual. People always want to know their future. They will visit palm readers, and for $9.99, the palm reader will tell you things that you want to hear. People consult horoscopes, astrologists, and tarot card readers as well.

Life was no different during the time of Jesus. There were various types of sages and wise men, magicians and scientists who said that they could predict the future. They were trained in science and in astronomy and tried to predict the various seasons of the years and the weather. There is a funny story in the Book of Acts where Paul and Barnabas were traveling through Ephesus, and while in the marketplace, they encountered a slave girl. She was possessed by a demon that gave her power to predict the future. Her owners were happy because people paid a lot of money to hear her predictions. When Paul heals the slave girl from her demonic possession, her owners run Paul and Barnabas out of town because they lost their primary source of income.

The slave girl was a false prophet. She was possessed by demons. Biblical prophets were different. Biblical prophets did not forecast the future like palm readers, rather, they looked around at the problems and pains, at the travesty of justice and wars and said to the people: if you continue what you are doing, you are headed towards destruction. God will come and destroy you. It is no different than a mom telling her daughter, if you continue not doing your homework and not studying hard, you will keep getting F's on your report card and most likely will not go to college. Then in a few years, when her daughter barely graduates high school and does not get into college, she could tell her friends that her mom *predicted* what would happen.

The Old Testament contains many writings from the prophets: Jonah, Isaiah, Jeremiah, Ezekiel, Amos, and Hosea among others. Some of these books are short and some are long, but they all looked around and saw the awful situation in which the people were in: wars, poverty, injustice, lack of compassion and realized that they needed to change as we hear in the following examples:

> "*Thus says the Lord: for three transgressions and for four I will not revoke the punishment; because they sell the righteous for silver, and the needy for a pair of sandals — they who trample the head of the poor into the dust of the earth, and push the afflicted out of the way (Amos 2:6–7).*

"Do not rejoice, O Israel! Do not exult as other nations do; for you have played the whore, departing from your God. You have loved a prostitute's pay on all threshing floors (Hosea 9:1).

Thus, says the Lord, Ah you shepherds of Israel who have been feeding yourselves! Should not shepherds feed the sheep? You eat the fat, you clothe yourselves with the wool, you slaughter the fatlings; but you do not feed the sheep (Ezekiel 34:2–3).

The Lord will roar from on high, and from His holy habitation utter His voice; He will roar mightily against His fold, and shout, like those who tread grapes, against all the inhabitants of the earth. The clamor will resound to the ends of the earth, for the Lord has an indictment against the nations; He is entering into judgment with all flesh (Jeremiah 25:30–31).

Draw near, O nations, to hear; O peoples, give heed! Let the earth hear, and all that fills it; the world, and all that comes from it. For the Lord is enraged against all the nations, and furious against all their hordes; he has doomed them, has given them over for slaughter. Their slain shall be cast out, and the stench of their corpses shall rise; the mountains shall flow with their blood. All the host of heaven shall rot away, and the skies roll up like a scroll. All their host shall wither like a leaf withering on a vine, or fruit withering on a fig tree (Isaiah 34:1–4).

There are many more examples from the prophetic writings. They all prophesy about caring for the poor, feeding the hungry, providing shelter for the homeless. When reading the prophetic writings, you might find that they repeat themselves often, and they certainly do, and for good reason. Children need constant reminders about cleaning their room, brushing their teeth, and taking out the garbage. Adults are no different. We need to be reminded about love, mercy, forgiveness, and compassion. The prophets continually remind the Israelites about following God and loving their neighbors.

Jesus came as a fulfillment of the prophetic preaching. Jesus' mission and ministry was to herald in the Kingdom of God and show people that there was an alternative way to live, where peace, justice, and mercy would reign and where there would be no more wars or fighting or injustice. Jesus begins His ministry in the Gospel of Mark with the simple phrase, "Repent for the Kingdom of God is at hand." Powerful words indeed! Yet, these words are easier said than done. More often than not I do not want to change. I like myself the way I am. Yet, Jesus reminds me that change is necessary. Change requires that I take a good long look at myself and I usually do not to do that. I would rather maintain the *status quo* and remain as I am.

Jesus went around the Galilee proclaiming this message of repentance. He preached against war and injustice. He spent most of His time with prostitutes, Samaritans, tax collectors, invalids, and the blind— people who were all considered outcasts of society. Jesus identified Himself with the poor, the hungry, the widow, and the infirm, people whom no one liked. He challenged the religious authorities and called them on their hypocrisy.

When we read the Old Testament, we also see that the Israelites did not take too kindly to the prophetic preaching. Who wants to hear about change? Who wants to leave their old ways behind and follow God? Change requires work and most of us do not want to do the work necessary to have our lives changed by God. It is no wonder why Jesus was threatened by the Jewish authorities and was eventually arrested. Preaching a message of repentance means that prophets will be persecuted and hated, yet that is what Jesus promised His disciples, "'Blessed are you when people revile you and persecute you and utter all kinds of evil against you falsely on my account. Rejoice and be glad, for your reward is great in heaven, for in the same way they persecuted the prophets who were before you" (Matt. 5:11–2).

Having a prophetic spirit means going against the grain, swimming upstream and not following the crowd. I am continually amazed at the vanity and rampant narcissism in our country; drug addicted rock stars, adulterous affairs in Hollywood, business people stealing and embezzling, it boggles the mind! It is rare, but once in a while, you hear about someone like Paul Newman or Jeff Bridges, mainstream Hollywood actors who dedicated their lives to the welfare of children, to the hungry, and to the poor and disadvantaged. You hear about the work and ministry of Jerry Lewis and children with muscular dystrophy and sports stars donating large sums of money to charity. You may hear these stories and quickly forget about them. Although one would not necessarily call Jerry Lewis or Paul Newman prophets, their actions, which are honorable and noble, refer to this same prophetic spirit that we encounter in the Scriptures; the notion that we dedicate our lives building up our brother and sister (what we would call the Body of Christ), and use our time, talents, and treasure for the goodwill of all. Actually, these are small ways that people can be prophetic, to live one's life not according to the ways of the world, but according to the ways of God.

Food For Thought

1. Set aside a few minutes each day and read some of the shorter prophetic books: Jonah, Amos, Hosea, and Micah. Take note of some themes or images that are repeated throughout the writings. Do specific themes or images come to mind?

2. Have you ever met someone who acts, thinks, or behaves 'differently' than the rest of the crowd? Does this bother you? What comes to mind when you see them?

3. The prophets did not conform to the generally accepted religion and social norms and customs of their time. They also were persecuted. Why do you think the world always wants people to 'conform' and 'fit in' with the rest of society?

4. For further reading: Luke 1:1–80, Matthew 5, Mark 1.

CHAPTER SIX

JESUS THE RABBI

Now when Jesus had finished saying these things, the crowds were astounded at his teaching, for he taught them as one having authority, and not as their scribes (Matt. 7:28–29).

E very day my daughters come home and tell me what they learned in school. They tell me about science experiments and tales about gym class and class trips. They tell me about circle time and reading. Every day my daughters bring home new information. I can see their excitement and joy in the way that they talk and share the events from the past day. Thankfully, my daughters enjoy school, and my wife and I encourage them to read and learn and grow. The more they learn, the more open they will be to the world around them. Learning is fun and we want to cultivate that love of learning every day.

When my daughters tell me about school, I cannot help but think about my own teachers. I was lucky to have dedicated teachers who loved and cared for us. They made learning fun. Dr. Carballo was one of my favorite college English teachers. Every class period he would come ready to teach. Dr. Carballo was a tough teacher, and some students did not like him because he was not an easy grader. He also demanded respect, and as his students, we had to earn it. I also remember my high school English teacher Mr. Fand, who taught British literature and Shakespeare. Like Dr. Caraballo, he had a love of learning that was contagious and carried over into the classroom. We acted out plays in the classroom and watched movies and films about the stories that we were reading in class.

Jesus was a teacher too. He taught people about God. He taught lessons about love, mercy, forgiveness, peace, justice, and kindness. He taught us about loving our neighbors and caring for those who were sick and suffering. Jesus taught not only by His words and but also by His actions. Some of Jesus' most famous sayings are contained in the Sermon on the Mount, a lengthy speech found in the Gospel of Matthew:

> *You are the salt of the earth; but if salt has lost its taste, how can its saltiness be restored? It is no longer good for anything but is thrown out and trampled under foot (Matt. 5:13).*

> *You have heard that it was said, "an eye for an eye and a tooth for a tooth" But I say to you, "Do*

no resist an evildoer. But if anyone strikes you on the right cheek, turn the other also; and if anyone wants to sue you and take your coat, give your cloak as well; if anyone forces you to go one mile, go also the second mile. Give to everyone who begs from you, and do not refuse anyone who wants to borrow from you (Matt. 5:38–42).

You have heard that it was said, "you shall love your neighbor and hate your enemy." But I say to you, Love your enemies and pray for those who persecute you, so that you may be children of your Father in heaven; for he makes his sun rise on the evil and on the good, and sends down rain on the righteous and on the unrighteous. (Matt 5:43–45).

Beware of practicing your piety before others in order to be seen by them; for then you have no reward from your Father in heaven (Matt 6:1).

Do not store up for yourselves treasures on earth, where moth and rust consume and where thieves break in and steal; but store up for yourselves treasures in heaven, where neither moth nor rust consumes and where thieves do not break in and steal. For where your treasure is, there your heart will be also. (Matt 6:19–21).

The Sermon on the Mount also includes the Lord's Prayer and other teachings about fasting, prayer, and almsgiving. The Sermon on the Mount is Jesus' first major teaching to His followers. Even though the Sermon on the Mount is only three chapters, it is central to our understanding of the Gospel. Jesus lays out His vision of how His followers should live and act.

Jesus also taught by His own personal example. He showed radical hospitality when He ate at the home of Zachaeus. It might not sound radical. After all, Jesus ate dinner with a lot of people. However, Zachaeus was a Jewish man who worked for the Roman government and most people would have considered being a traitor. Zachaeus was a Jew, yet he worked for the Roman government. Yet, Jesus did not care that Zachaeus was a tax collector. He wanted to spend time with Zachaeus and his family. Jesus broke a social custom and showed the people what God's love is all about. The fact that Jesus actually ate with sinners, outsiders, and those with social stigma shows that Jesus' command for the love of the neighbor is tantamount to discipleship. Eating and being with those whom society has pushed to the side is essential. God's love supersedes all things.

Jesus was a teacher who came just like Moses in the Old Testament. Moses taught the Israelites about God's love of the people and to follow His ways. Moses stood on Mount Sinai in order to receive the commands from God in the form of the Ten Commandments. These commandments were not just for Moses but for all the people. Many people look at Moses as the great deliverer since he led the Israelites across the Red Sea, yet it was Moses as teacher that is perhaps his most important role.

As most teachers, Jesus traveled throughout the Galilee area telling stories. People love stories. People remember the stories and tell and retell them throughout the generations. Every night before going to bed, I make sure to tell my daughters a bedtime story. Sometimes these stories are family stories that have been told and retold again and again or sometimes I read a story from a book. Sometimes I even make up stories. In any case, my girls, like all children young and old, enjoy a good story.

Jesus taught using stories as well. In the Bible, we call these stories parables. Parables are stories that are open ended, inviting the listener to contemplate the various aspects of the story. A parable does not offer neat and easy answers for life, rather the parable forces the listener to make a decision based on what they heard, and it requires thoughtful reflection and then action. Jesus taught using many such parables: the parable of the Sower, the parable of the Good Samaritan, the parable of the Rich Man and Lazarus as well as the parable of the Publican and the Pharisee just to name a few.

Furthermore, Jesus' teaching helped form and shape people into citizens of God's Kingdom. He wanted His followers live by His words not memorize a list of rules to follow. Here we need to go back to the Prophet Jeremiah. There is a passage early on in the Book of Jeremiah where Jeremiah describes God as a potter who shapes and forms Israel into a people. Just as a real potter shapes his clay on the spinning wheel, so too does God shape His people through the preaching of the Psalms, the Law, and the Prophets. This shaping is not a once and done event, but an ongoing one. Each and every day we are being formed and shaped into the people of God.

FOOD FOR THOUGHT

1. Take some time and make a list of your favorite teachers. Why are they so memorable?
   List their key characteristics or qualities. Give
   thanks to God for your teachers. They helped
   you get this far in life.

2. Take a few minutes and quickly read through
   the gospels. Which sayings or teachings of Jesus do you turn to again and again? Why? Do
   you have some favorite Bible verses?

3. My mom always told me that actions speak
   louder than words. It is one thing to say "you
   should love your friends," but if children do
   not see their parents being loving, how can
   they expect their children to show love? Do
   your actions reflect your core faith beliefs?
   How can you be a better example to your
   children or to those people around you?

4. For further reading: Psalm 119, Matthew
   5–7, Matthew 25, John 17.

CHAPTER SEVEN

JESUS THE LIGHT

As He walked along, He saw a man blind from birth. His disciples asked Him, 'Rabbi, who sinned, this man or his parents, that he was born blind?' Jesus answered, 'Neither this man nor his parents sinned; he was born blind so that God's works might be revealed in him. We must work the works of him who sent Me while it is day; night is coming when no one can work. As long as I am in the world, I am the light of the world.' When He had said this, He spat on the ground and made mud with the saliva and spread the mud on the man's eyes, saying to him, 'Go, wash in the pool of Siloam' (which means Sent). Then he went and washed and came back able to see (John 9:1–7).

Nighttime is scary for children. Nighttime usually means darkness, and darkness means ghosts and goblins and scary things that go bump in the night.

When I was a young boy, I was always scared of the dark. Mom bought me a nightlight that she plugged into the wall. I remember lying in my bed under the covers staring at the nightlight every night holding my stuffed white Snoopy doll. I knew that if I held my Snoopy nice and tight that I would be safe. I knew that the nightlight would keep all the badness away while I was sleeping. When morning comes, all is well again. The sun is shining and everything is okay.

In the opening passage of John's gospel, Jesus is referred to as the light of the world:

> *In the beginning was the Word, and the Word was with God, and the Word was God. He was in the beginning with God. All things came into being through Him, and without Him not one thing came into being. What has come into being in Him was life, and the life was the light of all people. The light shines in the darkness, and the darkness did not overcome it. There was a man sent from God, whose name was John. He came as a witness to testify to the light, so that all might believe through Him. He Himself was not the light, but He came to testify to the light. The true light, which enlightens everyone, was coming into the world (John 1:1–9).*

In the gospels, the world is often referred to as the darkness. Of course, we know that God made the world good and everything in it good. The Book of Genesis speaks about the plants, animals, and humans as being good. However, throughout the Scriptures, the world is also seen as broken and dark. From the very beginning of the Bible, we see Adam and Eve rejecting God and every generation after Adam and Eve seems to get worse. Cain murders Abel; the Israelites built the Tower of Babel, which they thought would reach heaven. The Book of Kings shows that people in power often abuse it at the expense of the poor and needy. The Bible shows us that people seem to reject God all the time. There are murders, scandals, adultery, and on and on it goes. It can be a very dark world out there.

Darkness is all around us. Just read the daily paper and you will read about the darkness: war, poverty, murder, financial, corruption, lying. Scandals are all around us from the highest levels of the Church to local government. There are days when I think, "Lord, can it get any worse than this?" and His answer is usually, "Yes." Yes? Yes! Just when we think that we heard it all, seen it all, and even done it all, life can get worse.

There is hope. In the Scriptures, light is seen as godly and good, revealing the evil of this world:

> *Do not rejoice over me, O my enemy; when I fall, I shall rise; when I sit in darkness, the Lord will be a light to me. I must bear the indignation of*

the Lord, because I have sinned against him, until he takes my side and executes judgment for me. He will bring me out to the light; I shall see his vindication. Then my enemy will see, and shame will cover her who said to me, 'Where is the Lord your God?' My eyes will see her downfall; now she will be trodden down like the mire of the streets (Micah 7:8–10).

The great day of the Lord is near, near and hastening fast; the sound of the day of the Lord is bitter, the warrior cries aloud there. That day will be a day of wrath, a day of distress and anguish, a day of ruin and devastation, a day of darkness and gloom, a day of clouds and thick darkness, a day of trumpet blast and battle cry against the fortified cities and against the lofty battlements. I will bring such distress upon people that they shall walk like the blind; because they have sinned against the Lord, their blood shall be poured out like dust, and their flesh like dung. Neither their silver nor their gold will be able to save them on the day of the Lord's wrath; in the fire of his passion the whole earth shall be consumed; for a full, a terrible end he will make of all the inhabitants of the earth (Zeph. 1:14–18).

The people who walked in darkness have seen a great light; those who lived in a land of deep darkness — on them light has shined. You have multiplied the nation, you have increased its joy; they rejoice before you as with joy at the harvest, as people exult when dividing plunder. For the yoke of their burden, and the bar across their shoulders, the rod of their oppressor, you have broken as on the day of Midian. For all the boots of the tramping warriors and all the garments rolled in blood shall be burned as fuel for the fire (Isaiah 9:2–5).

It is no wonder that Jesus is referred to as the light of the world. Jesus came into the world to reveal the light of God. Not only is Jesus the light of the world, He tells His disciples that since they are His followers, they too are to be lights to the world as well, "You are the light of the world. A city built on a hill cannot be hidden. No one after lighting a lamp puts it under the bushel basket, but on the lampstand, and it gives light to all in the house. In the same way, let your light shine before others, so that they may see your good works and give glory to your Father in heaven" (Matt. 5:14–16). When we share light, we are sharing the light of Jesus with others and making the world a little brighter. Certainly, the world needs more lights.

When I look around, I see that many people have shared their light with me: family, friends, neighbors, and pastors. They listened to my complaining and gave me consolation; they let me cry on their shoulders and gave me support when I am down. They send me notes and emails encouraging me to continue in the Lord's ministry. They surround me with God's love, care, and compassion. My friends, family, and neighbors have led me through terrible times and remind me that God is still good no matter what the world thinks. They remind me to cling to the light; otherwise, I will quickly fall back into darkness. The world needs more light, like the old Gospel hymn goes, "This little light of mine, I'm going to let it shine!" Are you up for the challenge? Are you going to let your light shine?

FOOD FOR THOUGHT

1. Take a moment and make a list of the different examples of darkness in the world and in your life. Are there things that you can do to help shine more light in the world?

2. Who are the 'lights' in your life? Why? What did they do to be lights to you?

3. How can you be a light to other people? Are there people in your life now who need more light?

4. For further reading: John 9, Matthew 5, Matthew 9.

CHAPTER EIGHT

JESUS THE RESURRECTION

But on the first day of the week, at early dawn, they came to the tomb, taking the spices that they had prepared. They found the stone rolled away from the tomb, but when they went in, they did not find the body. While they were perplexed about this, suddenly two men in dazzling clothes stood beside them. The women were terrified and bowed their faces to the ground, but the men said to them, 'Why do you look for the living among the dead? He is not here, but has risen. Remember how He told you, while He was still in Galilee, that the Son of Man must be handed over to sinners, and be crucified, and on the third day rise again.' Then they remembered His words, and returning from the tomb, they told all this to the eleven and to all the rest. Now it was Mary Magdalene, Joanna, Mary the mother of James, and the other women with them who told this to the apostles (Luke 24:1–10).

The Easter season is a joyful and wonderful time of year. I love the white Easter lilies and the fresh clean look of white vestments in Church. The Easter season also means Easter bonnets, Easter egg hunts and, of course, the Easter bunny. One cannot have Easter without the traditional Easter ham, served either cold or hot, with all the trimmings and, of course, lots and lots of Easter candy too. When I was little, my mom and dad always bought me a new tie or suit jacket for Easter. She wanted me to look my best on Easter Sunday. On one particular Easter Sunday, after my father parked the car in my grandparents' driveway, I ran straight to the backyard and plopped down right in middle of my brand new blue kiddy pool. Needless to say, mom was not happy. It was particularly hot that Easter, and I guess I just wanted to cool off after Church.

Easter is the foundation of our Christian faith: Jesus' death and resurrection. Every Sunday Christians around the world affirm and reaffirm our faith in the crucified and risen Lord as we recite the Nicene Creed, "He was crucified under Pontius Pilate, suffered and was buried. And the third day he rose again according to the Scriptures." Every Sunday is like a mini Easter; we celebrate Jesus' death and resurrection in the breaking of the bread. We share the good news of our new life together and leave, striving to serve both God and neighbor until the following week. We are fed and nourished on

Jesus' body and blood in order to proclaim the good news to the world.

Jesus' death and resurrection are found in each of the four gospels. Although the four accounts are different, they all agree on several points: that Jesus was betrayed by Judas Iscariot, that He was arrested in the Garden of Gethsemane, brought to the court of the High Priest, given both a Jewish and a Roman trial, and He was beaten, mocked, crucified, and placed in a tomb.

Most people do not realize that Jesus had two trials. Jesus was given a secular trial under the authority of Pontius Pilate, the Roman prefect of Judea. Judea was divided among several Roman governors who enforced Roman law and order. Pilate also assisted in collecting taxes, keeping general order, but deferred to the local Jewish leaders to enforce the Jewish laws. However, the Jewish leaders, under King Herod, enforced the Jewish laws and regulations. Both King Herod and Pontius Pilate found Jesus guilty of treason; He considered Himself to be the Son of God and a King, terms that went against the very grain of the religious and political culture of the time. Beginning with Caesar Augustus, the adopted son of Julius Caesar, the emperors were considered divine and deserved public worship and adoration. By referring to Jesus as the Son of God as well as King, it placed more importance on Jesus than it did on the Roman rulers. Therefore, according to the law, Jesus would be crucified. Ironically, even though the Jews and Romans did not like one another, the Gospel of Luke says that after Jesus' trial both Herod and Pilate became friends.

Executions are no longer public events as they were in previous centuries. Today executions are conducted under much scrutiny and are performed within the confines of prison walls with a handful of people: journalists, a few state witnesses, medical professionals, and state officials. In most states, prisoners are executed by lethal injection whereby the prisoner is strapped to a gurney and then injected with a potent dose of chemicals which eventually results in death. According to the medical profession, modern executions are nearly pain free, the prisoner first falls asleep and then their heart stops. They are dead.

However, crucifixion was a different matter altogether. One could imagine the humiliation of people jeering and mocking Jesus or any prisoner for that matter. The gospels say that Jesus carried His cross from the city of Jerusalem to just outside of the city to the place called Golgotha, the place of the skull. Luke says that Jesus was too weak to carry the cross beam so they implored Simeon of Cyrene, a visitor, to carry the cross for Jesus, "they compelled a passer-by, who was coming in from the country, to carry His cross; it was Simon of Cyrene, the father of Alexander and Rufus" (Mark 15:21).

When the procession left Jerusalem and came to the place where the crucifixion was going to take place, the Romans placed a sign above Jesus which was the judgment against Him: "Jesus the King of the Jews." John says that the sign was in Latin, Greek, and Hebrew, a shorthand way of saying it was placed in all languages. Latin was the common language of the Roman Empire; Greek was used throughout Palestine; and Hebrew was the language of the Old Testament. By saying that the sign was in these three languages, he is basically telling his readers that everyone in the entire Roman Empire, in the world, knows that Jesus was condemned as being the King of the Jews.

The gospels tell us that the soldiers nailed his hands and feet to the cross and then erected the cross-beam. Hanging from a cross meant that the prisoner could no longer breathe and after a few hours would die due to a lack of oxygen. It was common for crucifixions to be public events, which were similar to public hangings that occurred in our country in the 19th century. These were public spectacles, and people would come out to see the prisoners. John tells us that His favorite disciple John the Beloved and His mother Mary was at the foot of the cross; however, Mark tells us that the disciples and the women looked on from afar, meaning that they did not come close.

Then Jesus died. According to the gospels, that day was the evening of the Sabbath so the bodies could not be left on the cross. Therefore, Joseph of

Arimathea asked Pilate to have Jesus' body. Joseph of Arimathea is only mentioned a few times in the gospels and only in relation to Jesus' death. Luke mentions that Joseph was a member of the Jewish council but did not go along with their plans. He asked Pilate for the body of Jesus and "wrapped it in a linen cloth, and laid it in a rock-hewn tomb where no one had been laid. It was the day of Preparation, and the Sabbath was beginning (Luke 23:53–54). The gospels also testify to the fact that Joseph rolled a stone in front of the tomb and then left.

Matthew states that the tomb belonged to Joseph of Armithaea who gave up his family tomb so that Jesus could be put into it. The Evangelists also agree that when the myrhhbearing women came to the tomb on that first Easter Sunday, they encountered the risen Lord. Later that same day, in the Upper Room in Jerusalem, the risen Lord appeared to the disciples:

> *When it was evening on that day, the first day of the week, and the doors of the house where the disciples had met were locked for fear of the Jews, Jesus came and stood among them and said, 'Peace be with you.' After He said this, He showed them His hands and His side. Then the disciples rejoiced when they saw the Lord. Jesus said to them again, 'Peace be with you. As the Father has sent Me, so I send you.' When He had said this, He breathed on them and said to them,*

'Receive the Holy Spirit. If you forgive the sins of
any, they are forgiven them; if you retain the sins
of any, they are retained' (John 20:19–23).

A few important things are worth mentioning. While His body was different, they still were able to recognize Him. Yet, at the same time, He still had the wounds in His hands and the mark in His side from the crucifixion. In other words, the resurrection did not erase those marks. Likewise Jesus had the ability to eat with His disciples, and on two occasions, we know that He broke bread with them.

According to the Book of Acts, we know that for forty days the risen Lord appeared to His disciples and continued to teach them about the Kingdom of God. Eventually, He took them outside of Jerusalem to the village called Bethany, the same place where Jesus raised Lazarus from the dead, and He blessed His disciples, telling them to stay in the city until they receive the gift of the Holy Spirit. Then Jesus ascended into heaven. Jesus ascended so that His disciples could continue his preaching and teaching ministry.

These resurrection events are full of wonder and awe. We hear about the cross, the tomb, and the resurrection. We hear about Jesus breaking bread with His disciples. We tend to go through the same motions year after year: Church services, an Easter ham dinner, and an egg hunt. We do not give Easter a second glance. We forget that Easter is foundational to our faith as we hear in the writings of the Apostle Paul, "But in fact, Christ has been raised from the dead, the first fruits of those who have died. For since death came through a human being, the resurrection of the dead has also come through a human being; for all die in Adam, so all will be made alive in Christ" (1 Cor. 15:20). Paul promises us that just as Jesus was raised from the dead by the glory of God so too will we be raised from the dead too.

Throughout His ministry, Jesus preached new life. We tend to go through life trying to earn brownie points with God thinking that the more money we give to the Church or the more Church services we attend or the more we volunteer for a local outreach ministry that somehow we will earn points so that we will get into heaven at a later date. God does not need our brownie points! God loves us with an abundant love. All that God wants from us is to worship Him and love Him with all our mind, soul, heart, and strength. Any good that we do or will do in the future flows from our love of God. In other words, the good deeds and actions that we do comes from our love of God, our actions are love being shared with other people.

FOOD FOR THOUGHT

1. Take time and slowly read the four resurrection accounts. Make a list of some of the things that the risen Lord did and said after He was raised from the dead. Does anything in particular stay with you as you read the passages?

2. Did you know that every Sunday we actually celebrate a "mini-Easter." Every Sunday we gather as the Body of Christ to break bread and recall Jesus' last words to His disciples.

3. For further reading: Mark 16, John 21, Luke 24, Matthew 28.

CHAPTER NINE

JESUS THE JUDGE

I can do nothing on My own authority; as I hear, I judge; and My judgment is just, because I seek not My own will but the will of Him who sent Me" (John 5:30).

Many people are drawn to courtroom television shows like *Court TV* or *Judge Judy*, or if they enjoy good fiction, they will read an Agatha Christie, John Grisham, or Sue Grafton crime novel. When I was still living at home, my parents liked to watch a lot of court related programs: *Matlock, Night Court,* and *Law and Order.* Mom would watch *The Peoples' Court* when she came home from work. People love courtroom drama. Millions of people watched the O.J. Simpson murder trial and just recently people are watching the Casey Anthony murder trial. I think people like these programs because it shows the best and worst of humanity, they reveal the need for order and justice while at the same time show people fighting for their innocence. There is intrigue, secrecy, suspicion, suspense, all the ingredients for a good story. It is no wonder why John Grisham has sold so many books! People love court cases whether on the small screen at home, on the movie screen in a theater, or in a book.

The Old Testament speaks about God as a judge. God shows us mercy, love, and compassion. Divine justice is supposed to overrule the often misappropriated justice that we have. Our justice system is supposed to work but quite often depending on the lawyers, prosecutor, or jury, sometimes things fall apart.

Jesus also referred to as a judge, yet some of His teachings may sound like He contradicts Himself, especially when we hear a passage such as the following:

> *Jesus said to them, 'Very truly, I tell you, the Son can do nothing on His own, but only what He sees the Father doing; for whatever the Father does, the Son does likewise. The Father loves the Son and shows Him all that He Himself is doing; and He will show Him greater works than these, so that you will be astonished. Indeed, just as the Father raises the dead and gives them life, so also the Son gives life to whomsoever He wishes. The Father judges no one but has given all judgement to the Son, so that all may honour the Son just as they honour the Father. Anyone who does not honor the Son does not honor the Father who*

*sent Him. Very truly, I tell you, anyone who
hears My word and believes Him who sent Me
has eternal life, and does not come under judge-
ment, but has passed from death to life.*

*'Very truly, I tell you, the hour is coming, and
is now here, when the dead will hear the voice
of the Son of God, and those who hear will live.
For just as the Father has life in Himself, so He
has granted the Son also to have life in Himself;
and He has given Him authority to execute judgment, because He is the Son of Man. Do not be
astonished at this; for the hour is coming when
all who are in their graves will hear His voice and
will come out — those who have done good, to
the resurrection of life, and those who have done
evil, to the resurrection of condemnation. 'I can
do nothing on My own. As I hear, I judge; and
My judgment is just, because I seek to do not My
own will but the will of Him who sent Me (John
5:19–30).*

With a quick read of the passages above, Jesus
sounds like a politician. On the one hand, Jesus says
that the Father has given all authority to Him and
then, on the other hand, He says that He is a judge
but He does not judge. What is going on here? He
sounds like He is talking out two sides of his mouth.
It is no different than when a teacher grades end of

the year exams. If a student follows the syllabus and does all the readings and does well on the exams, then he will receive top grades. His judgment by the teacher is not something out of the blue but an affirmation of the students work. Likewise, a poor student will receive a bad mark. In a way, the student, whether the good student or the poor student judged themselves in that by either doing the work or not doing the work they reaped their own reward. The point that Jesus makes is that since He is the Son of God, all authority and power and judgment has been given over to Him and, therefore, He will serve as the judge on that great and final day.

Another example, also from the gospels, reveals the same idea. Towards the end of the Gospel of Matthew, we hear the following words:

> 'When the Son of Man comes in His glory, and all the angels with Him, then He will sit on the throne of His glory. All the nations will be gathered before Him, and He will separate people one from another as a shepherd separates the sheep from the goats, and He will put the sheep at His right hand and the goats at the left. Then the king will say to those at His right hand, "Come, you that are blessed by My Father, inherit the kingdom prepared for you from the foundation of the world; for I was hungry and you gave Me food, I was thirsty and you gave Me something to drink,

I was a stranger and you welcomed Me, I was naked and you gave Me clothing, I was sick and you took care of Me, I was in prison and you visited Me." Then the righteous will answer Him, "Lord, when was it that we saw You hungry and gave You food, or thirsty and gave You something to drink? And when was it that we saw You a stranger and welcomed You, or naked and gave You clothing? And when was it that we saw You sick or in prison and visited You?" And the king will answer them, "Truly I tell you, just as you did it to one of the least of these who are members of My family, you did it to Me." Then He will say to those at His left hand, "You that are accursed, depart from Me into the eternal fire prepared for the devil and his angels; for I was hungry and you gave Me no food, I was thirsty and you gave Me nothing to drink, I was a stranger and you did not welcome Me, naked and you did not give Me clothing, sick and in prison and you did not visit Me." Then they also will answer, "Lord, when was it that we saw You hungry or thirsty or a stranger or naked or sick or in prison, and did not take care of You?" Then He will answer them, "Truly I tell you, just as you did not do it to one of the least of these, you did not do it to Me." And these will go away into eternal punishment, but the righteous into eternal life' (Matt. 25:31–46).

This passage speaks about the Son of Man acting as a judge. However, when reading this passage, make sure to notice that the judgment is not an arbitrary one, but a judgment based on love. The sheep were the ones who served and cared for the prisoner, the sick, clothed the naked, and gave food and drink to those who were hungry and thirsty. The other group, which Matthew calls the goats, did not do these things. As you can see, the real judgment is based on loving the neighbor. The Son of Man just affirms or acknowledges what has been done or not done; He is not out to get anyone. Unfortunately, we tend to forget that the greatest commandment is love. Numerous times in the New Testament Jesus says that love is the greatest commandment.

When I was very young, I used to think of God as an old man with a white beard sitting at a big desk with two long lists: one list had all the good things I had done and the other had a list of all the bad things I had done. I thought God was watching my every move, and one wrong step and zap He would get me with a bolt of lighting. Actually, many children think this way. It is a normal development in the spiritual life. However, when reading the gospels, we see that the God of Jesus, whom we call our Father, is not out to zap us. Our God is a god of mercy and compassion, even though we do not always see it this way.

A good example is the story about Jonah and the whale. God sends Jonah to preach to the people of

Nineveh. They are being very wicked and nasty. God wants the Ninevites to repent and, therefore, He sends Jonah as the prophet to speak to them. Jonah is scared so he gets on the first ship going to Tarshish, a city far away from Nineveh. All of a sudden, while the ship is at sea, a great storm arises, the sailors are scared, they might die. In order to appease the gods, they throw Jonah over board and a big fish, or whale, swallows Jonah. For three days and three nights, Jonah stays in the belly of the fish. Then the fish spits up Jonah on the shore, and Jonah eventually travels to Nineveh preaching the Gospel. Jonah thinks it is a lost cause. They are so wicked and evil they will never repent. Jonah is wrong. The king realizes how far they are from God's love. They change their wicked ways and repent from the evil. One would think that Jonah would be happy, thrilled, excited! After all, these very bad people who were wicked and evil now changed their ways. Yet, Jonah is angry! He wants God to punish them for their bad behavior. Jonah does not want the Ninevites to get off with a little slap on the wrist. He wants punishment. He wants revenge. Yet, God tells him in the end, "And should I not be concerned about Nineveh, that great city, in which there are more than a hundred and twenty thousand people who do not know their right hand from their left, and also many animals?" (Jonah 4:11). God's last word to Jonah is striking. When all is said and done, God has love and concern for these Ninevites. He accepts their repentance as genuine and forgives them. Yet, Jonah cannot accept this. He wants God to zap the Ninevites.

Revenge is sweet. Many times if someone cuts me off on the highway or makes me angry, my first inclination is to do the same to them—to get them back! As our default position, our first instinct usually is to get them back, to do to them what they do to us. Yet, this is not the Jesus way. Jesus reminds us that we are not supposed to retaliate but to always show love and compassion. Jonah's problem was that he was short sighted. He did not see the big picture, that after all those years of wickedness they changed their ways for the good. Jonah wanted God to repay evil for evil. The story of Jonah shows us that our God is a compassionate God who loves and cares for His people, something which I find hard to understand, yet I am reminded of every time I read Jonah and the whale.

FOOD FOR THOUGHT

1. Do you consider yourself a judgmental person? If so, how can you change?

2. Take time to read the story of Jonah. Make a note of the images or phrases that move you? What do you think of the ending?

3. Next time you are tempted to judge someone, remember that only God is the judge. According to the Apostle Paul, we are not even supposed to judge ourselves!

4. For further reading: Psalm 7, Psalm 96, Matthew 7:1–5, John 7:20–25.

CHAPTER TEN

JESUS THE CHRIST

Jesus went on with His disciples to the villages of Caesarea Philippi; and on the way, He asked His disciples, 'Who do people say that I am?' And they answered Him, 'John the Baptist; and others, Elijah; and still others, one of the prophets.' He asked them, 'But who do you say that I am?' Peter answered Him, 'You are the Messiah.' And He sternly ordered them not to tell anyone about Him (Mark 8:27–30).

Many people think that Jesus Christ is a name just like Bill Mills or Jane Doe, His first name being Jesus and His family name being Christ. After all, it seems quite logical. Everyone has both a first name like Bill and a second name like Mills. However, in the ancient world, people were known by their role in life such as Bill the Baker or Susan the Seamstress. Eventually, their names would be shortened to Bill Baker or Susan Seamstress.

However, the name Jesus Christ is a different. The name Jesus is the Greek version of the Hebrew name Yeshua, which means "God saves." Yeshua is translated into English as Joshua. According to the Old Testament, we know that after Moses died, Joshua became the leader of the Israelites and it was Joshua who led the people across the Red Sea into the Promised Land.

The name Christ is from the Greek word *Christos*, which is the translation of the Hebrew word messiah. The word messiah means to smear with oil, and the secondary meaning is the anointed one. Why would Jesus be called the anointed one? Eventually Jesus' followers were known as Christians or followers of Christ as we hear in the book of Acts, "and it was in Antioch that the disciples were first called 'Christians.'"

In the Old Testament, the prophet was the one who anointed the king. Anointing was a both a religious and public way of making a new king. The word messiah means the anointed one, and the king was supposed to be the anointed one of God who would take care of God's people. In the Old Testament, the Prophet Samuel anointed King David to be the new King of Israel. The Gospel of Luke says that Jesus was anointed:

When He came to Nazareth, where He had been brought up, He went to the synagogue on the sabbath day, as was His custom. He stood up

> *to read, and the scroll of the Prophet Isaiah was given to Him. He unrolled the scroll and found the place where it was written: 'The Spirit of the Lord is upon me, because he has anointed me to bring good news to the poor. He has sent me to proclaim release to the captives and recovery of sight to the blind, to let the oppressed go free, to proclaim the year of the Lord's favor' (Luke 4:16–19).*

Jesus begins His public ministry by quoting the Prophet Isaiah (61:1–2), a portion towards the end of the book where Isaiah describes the Jubilee year as the release of captives and recovery of sight to the blind, to let the oppressed go free, to proclaim the year of the Lord's favor. In ancient Israel, the Jubilee year was a year when all debts and payments were cancelled. According to the religious calendar, there was a cycle of thirty-nine years, the fortieth year was a special year where the Jews would donate a portion of their crops to the poor and would release all debts that someone owed them. In a way, the Jubilee year was a way that the Jews reminded themselves of God's goodness and grace, that they practiced what God was continually doing all the time.

The messiah was supposed to restore God's Kingdom and bring about justice, mercy, and peace. Some people, even Jesus' closest friends, had trouble realizing that Jesus was the messiah. At one point, Jesus' best friend and relative, John the Baptist was in prison and told his disciples, "Are you the one who is to come or are we to wait for another?" (Matt. 11:3). Jesus responds to John's disciples, "Go and tell John what you hear and see: the blind receive their sight, the lame walk, the lepers are cleansed, the deaf hear, the dead are raised, and the poor have good news brought to them. And blessed is anyone who takes no offense at Me" (Matt. 11:4-6).

Jesus begins His public ministry by being baptized by John the Baptist. Baptism is a type of anointing; John anointed Jesus just like the Prophet Samuel anointed David. One day Jesus saw John baptizing in the Jordan River, and He told John that He also wanted to be baptized. John was hesitant by saying, "I need to be baptized by You, and do You come to me?" in other words, how can John baptize Jesus? Yet, John goes along with it and a voice from heaven affirms this baptism by saying, "This is my Son, the Beloved, with whom I am well pleased" (Matt. 3:17).

I know many people who like to keep Jesus at an arm's length distance; after all, we do not let God to get close to us. We do not want Jesus coming close because he may require us to change our lives or have our lives changed. We like the *status quo*; we like how things are, why should we change? Yet, in our baptism, we are also anointed by the grace of the Holy Spirit. At our baptism, we die with Jesus and we are raised for new life in Him. As the Apostle Paul says, as many as are baptized into Christ have put on Christ. Putting on Christ is being anointed by Him and means that we have the same power to change peoples' lives. Jesus tells His disciples that even if they have the smallest amount of faith, even as small as a mustard seed that they could move mountains!

Food For Thought

1. Most of us were too young to remember our baptism. Our baptism was the beginning of our journey of faith. Take time and reflect upon what baptism means, especially in light of this chapter and the various scripture references made to it.

2. When we were baptized, we "put on Christ," as St. Paul says in his epistles. Putting on Christ is awe-inspiring but also means that we have work to do. When we put on Christ, it means that we become the hands and feet of Christ to the world. What prevents you from serving others? How can you serve others better in the coming weeks and months?

3. The word 'Christian' means follower of Christ. Do not forget that when people meet you, they are meeting an ambassador of the Church, now that is food for thought for a lifetime!

4. For further reading: Matthew 3:1–17; Mark 1:1–13; Luke 3:21–22; John 3:22–30.

CHAPTER ELEVEN

JESUS THE LAMB

The next day he saw Jesus coming towards him and declared, 'Here is the Lamb of God who takes away the sin of the world! This is He of whom I said, "After me comes a man who ranks ahead of me because He was before me." I myself did not know Him, but I came baptizing with water for this reason, that He might be revealed to Israel.' And John testified, 'I saw the Spirit descending from heaven like a dove, and it remained on Him. I myself did not know Him, but the One who sent me to baptize with water said to me, "He on whom you see the Spirit descend and remain is the one who baptizes with the Holy Spirit." And I myself have seen and have testified that this is the Son of God' (John 1:29–34).

It might seem strange that the gospels speak of Jesus as both a shepherd and a lamb at the same time. When we read scripture, we must remember that Matthew, Mark, Luke, and John used a wide range of images and metaphors. Both of these images, Jesus as the Good Shepherd as well as Jesus as the Lamb of God, apply to Jesus and His ministry.

In the ancient world, as in many rural parts of the world today, shepherds tend sheep. Today in Galilee and throughout Israel, you will see older Bedouin tribesmen with a flock or two of sheep. Sheep are raised for their wool, which is eventually shorn and woven into wool for making shirts, sweaters, shawls, pants, or other clothes, and they are also raised for their meat, especially lamb kebabs on the grill, leg of lamb in the oven, or lamb patties on pita bread. The smell is overpowering too. You can eat your way through North Africa and the Middle East just by eating a variety of lamb dishes.

In ancient Israel, lambs were used in religious ceremonies. The Jews had a cycle of festival celebrations, which marked the different liturgical seasons in life, the most important one being Passover. At Passover, the Jews were supposed to sacrifice a lamb as we see in this passage from Exodus:

> *The Lord said to Moses and Aaron in the land of Egypt: This month shall mark for you the beginning of months; it shall be the first month of the year for you. Tell the whole congregation of Israel that on the tenth of this month they are to take a*

lamb for each family, a lamb for each household. If a household is too small for a whole lamb, it shall join its closest neighbor in obtaining one; the lamb shall be divided in proportion to the number of people who eat of it. Your lamb shall be without blemish, a year-old male; you may take it from the sheep or from the goats. You shall keep it until the fourteenth day of this month; then the whole assembled congregation of Israel shall slaughter it at twilight. They shall take some of the blood and put it on the two doorposts and the lintel of the houses in which they eat it. They shall eat the lamb that same night; they shall eat it roasted over the fire with unleavened bread and bitter herbs. Do not eat any of it raw or boiled in water, but roasted over the fire, with its head, legs, and inner organs. You shall let none of it remain until the morning; anything that remains until the morning you shall burn. This is how you shall eat it: your loins girded, your sandals on your feet, and your staff in your hand; and you shall eat it hurriedly. It is the passover of the Lord. For I will pass through the land of Egypt that night, and I will strike down every firstborn in the land of Egypt, both human beings and animals; on all the gods of Egypt I will execute judgments: I am the Lord. The blood shall be a sign for you on the houses where you live: when I see the blood, I will pass over you, and no plague shall destroy you when I strike the land of Egypt (Exodus 12:1–13).

One could just imagine the smell and stench of lambs slaughtered in the temple, lambs crying in their pens, and people jostling and fighting for the best cut of lamb for their evening meal. According to the Old Testament laws, the Temple priests were permitted to keep a portion of the lamb and the rest would go to the person who made the offering. Since everyone had to have a lamb at Passover, this meant that the farmers did very good business selling and slaughtering these lambs.

Jesus' cousin and best friend, John the Baptist, publicly proclaimed Jesus as the Lamb of God, "Behold the lamb of God who takes away the sins of the world" (John 1:28). Furthermore, according to the final events of Jesus' life, John tells us that Jesus was being crucified at the same time that the lambs were being slaughtered in Jerusalem for the great Passover Feast, echoing a passage by Isaiah:

Surely he has borne our infirmities and carried our diseases; yet we accounted him stricken, struck down by God, and afflicted. But he was wounded for our transgressions, crushed for our iniquities; upon him was the punishment that made us whole, and by his bruises we are healed. All we like sheep have gone astray; we have all turned to our own way, and the Lord has laid on him the iniquity of us all.

He was oppressed, and he was afflicted, yet he did not open his mouth; like a lamb that is led to the slaughter, and like a sheep that before its shearers is silent, so he did not open his mouth. By a perversion of justice he was taken away. Who could have imagined his future? For he was cut off from the land of the living, stricken for the transgression of my people. They made his grave with the wicked and his tomb with the rich, although he had done no violence, and there was no deceit in his mouth (Isaiah 53:4–9).

Isaiah speaks here of the Messiah, the redeemer of Israel who would come as the Suffering Servant rather than a glorious earthly king. The Messiah would not come as a powerful military leader on horses and chariots with soldiers and power, but He would come humbly and quietly. Additionally, He would suffer for the nation of Israel as these passages clearly show. We know from the four gospel accounts that Jesus suffered mocking, scourging, humiliation, public jeering, yet never defended Himself from His accusers. Jesus went willingly to His death, allowing the powers and authorities have their own false justice. Jesus was put to death just as the priests in the Temple were killing all of the Passover lambs for the feast.

Yet, even in His crucifixion, Jesus is victorious. The Book of Revelation calls Jesus the slain lamb, a term that is used over twenty times, reminding readers that ultimately, it is the slain lamb who reigns supreme over the powers and authorities of the world.

FOOD FOR THOUGHT

1. It is hard to hear the small still voice of Jesus in this very loud world of ours. Each and every day make sure to spend some quiet time in meditation or reflection, thinking of how you and your family can be better disciples.

2. Sheep naturally follow the shepherd. They follow where the food is. Wherever the shepherd goes, the sheep follow. Do you always follow Jesus? What usually gets in the way of following Him? Do you prevent others from following Jesus?

3. Your priest or pastor is the shepherd of your local parish flock. Being a pastor is not an easy job. If possible, try to help your pastor, offering your time, talents, and treasure, so His burden can be lifted. Shepherds cannot do all the work themselves, even St. Paul had coworkers!

4. For further reading: Ezekiel 34, Jeremiah 23:1–6, John 10, Ephesians 2:11–22.

CHAPTER TWELVE

JESUS THE VINE

I am the vine, you are the branches. Those who abide in Me and I in them bear much fruit, because apart from Me, you can do nothing. Whoever does not abide in Me is thrown away like a branch and withers; such branches are gathered, thrown into the fire, and burned. If you abide in Me, and My words abide in you, ask for whatever you wish, and it will be done for you. My Father is glorified by this, that you bear much fruit and become My disciples. As the Father has loved Me, so I have loved you; abide in My love. If you keep My commandments, you will abide in My love, just as I have kept my Father's commandments and abide in His love. I have said these things to you so that My joy may be in you, and that your joy may be complete (John 15:5–11).

I enjoy a glass of wine with dinner, especially if we have company or during other special events. Other times I will have a glass while watching a movie or while sitting and talking with my wife. I enjoy wine, especially a full-bodied red wine, like a Bordeaux, Cabernet, or Malbec. Over the years, I really have appreciated wine making. The wine making process is a long one, from planting and tending the vineyard, to harvesting and processing the grapes, from bottling and labeling the wine, letting it rest, and then sending it for shipping. Many people are involved in the wine making process.

One year my family traveled to northern California for a one-day wine tasting tour. We drove up and down the Sonoma and Napa Valley stopping in several wineries. The landscape was beautiful and reminded me of northern Italy, gently rolling hills, small rivers and streams slowly snaking through the valleys, and, of course, miles and miles of vineyards. Every town in northern California had several wineries, some big and some small, some old, and others new. You could spend an entire week visiting and tasting wine.

One of Jesus' most interesting titles is Jesus the Vine. In the fifteenth chapter of John's gospel, He refers to Himself as the vine:

> *"I am the true vine, and My Father is the vine-grower. He removes every branch in Me that bears*

no fruit. Every branch that bears fruit He prunes to make it bear more fruit. You have already been cleansed by the word that I have spoken to you. Abide in Me as I abide in you. Just as the branch cannot bear fruit by itself unless it abides in the vine, neither can you unless you abide in Me. I am the vine, you are the branches. Those who abide in me and I in them bear much fruit, because apart from Me, you can do nothing. Whoever does not abide in Me is thrown away like a branch and withers; such branches are gathered, thrown into the fire, and burned. If you abide in Me and My words abide in you, ask for whatever you wish, and it will be done for you. My Father is glorified by this, that you bear much fruit and become My disciples (John 15:1–11).

This passage comes towards the end of Jesus' life. He is headed towards Jerusalem and his approaching death. Jesus instructs His disciples to abide or remain with Him, a word that appears eight times in this short passage. Jesus reminds His disciples that if they remain with Him, then they will bear fruit. If they do not abide with Him, they will not bear fruit. Reading this passage brings to mind one of those wiry spindly vines that meander through vineyards. Wine vines take between seven or eight years actually to produce wine quality grapes. The vines need to mature and strengthen and become strong enough to produce clusters of grapes. You can have the most beautiful plot of land and strong green vines, but if you do not have grapes, well, you will not have wine.

At the end of the passage, Jesus speaks about bearing fruit. Of course, He is not talking about literal grapes like merlot, chardonnay, or cabernet, but rather spiritual fruit. Jesus' followers are supposed to grow fruits of the Spirit, which are enumerated by Paul's letter to the Galatians, "The fruit of the Spirit is love, joy, peace, patience, kindness, generosity, faithfulness, gentleness, and self-control" (Gal. 5:22). These are very good fruits. After all, who does not want love, joy, and peace? However, cultivating fruit is not easy. If you think it is hard growing grapes, try growing spiritual fruits, it is even harder!

My fallen human nature would rather be angry, grumpy, and selfish rather than being caring, kind, and faithful. There are times when I want to be stingy and say what is on my mind without caring how the other person reacts. Being a Christian is not easy. It is much easier to be mean, angry, and selfish. Try being nice to someone in the grocery store who cuts in front of you at the checkout counter or who cuts in front of you while driving and see how kind you are or try being patient when your four-year-old is whining about his toy that you took away because he was hitting his brother, not easy! Every day I find myself failing and falling down. I constantly wind up doing the opposite of what I am supposed to be doing.

When reading the scripture passage above, I am reminded that grapes can only grow if they remain as part of the vine. They cannot grow by themselves. In order for grapes to grow, they need vitamins, nutrients, water, and energy. The vine is like an umbilical cord that connects the grapes to the main food source, just like a fetus is connected to its mother in the womb. The umbilical cord is very important and provides real life to the baby, without it the baby would die. If I cut myself off from Jesus, I will spiritually die. I know that He gives me life. Abiding or remaining with Jesus is the life force that keeps me going, keeps me alive each and every day.

FOOD FOR THOUGHT

1. Jesus commands His disciples to bear fruit. St. Paul says the same thing but emphasizes the "fruit of the Spirit." Do you find it difficult to cultivate fruit?

2. Re-read the passage from the Apostle Paul's letter to the Galatians. Are there any fruits that you are growing right now? Are there fruits that come easy to you?

3. Being part of the vine reminds us that we are part of a much larger community of faith. Very often we might feel lonely and isolated, but in actuality, we are all members of one another. When one suffers, we all suffer. When one rejoices, we all rejoice. I always find comfort when I reflect on the Church being a vineyard with all the vines intermingling and growing up together.

4. For further reading: Isaiah 5:1–11, Jeremiah 2:21, Ezekiel 19:10-14, 1 Corinthians 12.

CHAPTER THIRTEEN

JESUS THE FRIEND
OF THE POOR

"Blessed are the poor in spirit, for theirs in the kingdom of heaven" (Matt. 11:5).

Even though the United States is the wealthiest country in the world with hundreds of Fortune 500 companies and large corporations, we have too much poverty. Our country has the best military and armed forces in the world, some of the best universities and colleges, and yet we still have poor people. Visit any large city in America, and you will certainly encounter homelessness and urban poor. Every day across the country, people line up in bread lines and in soup kitchens waiting for a hot meal and a cup of coffee. Others wait for food stamps and clothes. Others wait in line for help with rent or paying their bills. Poverty is not just for city people either. Rural parts of our country are also affected by poverty too, and in many ways, the rural poor are worse off, because they lack many resources which inner cities have such as buses, food banks, and soup kitchens. However, if you live in a trailer park out in the country areas and have no car or means of transportation, you are really in trouble. Likewise, you will have to drive a long way to find food, clothing, shelter, and other resources.

When we think of poverty, we usually think of material poverty: street people, homeless, vagabonds walking the streets. However, there is also another type of poverty too: spiritual poverty. Material poverty is visible. However, spiritual poverty often goes undetected. There are couples who are married yet live in quiet desperation because their spouse may not be as loving and caring as they should or people fall into spiritual despair and despondency. People lack hope in God and fall into severe depression. Some even fall further into despair and commit suicide, the ultimate act of hopelessness. Spiritual poverty is just as bad as material poverty if not worse; it usually goes on undetected, and people often find it difficult to reach out and get help.

According to the gospels, we know that Jesus was born in poverty. The Gospel of Matthew tells us that Jesus was born in Bethlehem, a village near the Galilee area. The gospels state that after Jesus was born, he was placed in a manger, which is basically a food trough for animals. Eventually, Mary and Joseph took Jesus to Nazareth where he was raised among very poor people: day laborers, poor farmers, and peasants. Furthermore, from what the Gospels tell us, Jesus had no real home of his own. Jesus devoted His entire life to the poor. He spent His time with the poor, the lame, the blind, those who were outcasts in society. One would think that Jesus would spend His time with the rich and wealthy, those who had material possessions, but He did the opposite. Jesus accused the rich of not being able to follow Him because of their possessions. At one point in the Gospel, a rich man meets Jesus and wants to follow Him. The rich man asks Jesus what is the greatest commandment and Jesus responds by saying, "If you wish to enter life, keep the commandments" (Matt. 19:17). Then Jesus told the rich man, "If you wish to be perfect, go, sell your possessions, and give the money to the poor, and you will have treasure in heaven; then come follow Me" (Matt. 19:21–22). Easier said than done! The man could not do what Jesus asked him, and he left which then inspires Jesus to conclude this passage by saying:

> *"Then Jesus said to His disciples, 'Truly I tell you, it will be hard for a rich person to enter the kingdom of heaven. Again I tell you, it is easier for a camel to go through the eye of a needle than for someone who is rich to enter the kingdom of God.' When the disciples heard this, they were greatly astounded and said, 'Then who can be saved?' But Jesus looked at them and said, 'For mortals it is impossible, but for God all things are possible"* (Matt. 19:23–26).

The problem is simple. The rich and wealthy are more interested in keeping their resources than sharing them. Of course, not all wealthy people are stingy and greedy. I have met some who were very always the case, and not every rich person is self-centered and selfish, yet wealth and money are often big temptations. Jesus reminds us that we are supposed to build up treasures in heaven where moth and rust do not consume or where thieves break in and steal but rather to store up treasures in heaven (Matt. 6:19–21). Later in the same passage, Jesus tells His disciples, "You cannot serve God and wealth" (Matt. 6:24). There are other similar passages where Jesus speaks out against riches and wealth. Of course, it is not sinful to have material resources, but Jesus does expect us to share what we have with those who are less fortunate. In other words, Jesus all wants us to be philanthropists. Philanthropy comes from the Greek word, which means *lover of mankind* or *lover of humanity*. We often hear about rich people who donate money for new buildings or who donate money for medical or science research. These very wealthy people are called philanthropists, because they are caring for their fellow brothers and sisters. They are caring for the people around them.

All these examples remind us of God's love for the poor. Why? Because the poor are the ones who have nothing. Money opens doors in our culture. If you have money, you have instant access to material goods, resources, and job opportunities, networking, and other benefits. If you are poor, you have a much harder time getting ahead in life.

Christians are called to serve the poor. Mother Teresa said that when she looked at someone who was poor, she saw the face of Christ. When she gave a cup of water or a bowl of soup to a homeless woman in Calcutta, she was serving Christ. There are other people like Mother Teresa, both in East and West, some clergy and others laity who devoted themselves to the poor. Father Damian Molokai volunteered to go to Hawaii, where he served a leper colony, knowing that one day he may contact leprosy himself and die. St. Herman of Alaska left the comforts of his Russian Orthodox monastery in northern Russia and cared for the poor, the orphans, and the widows in Alaska. Jean Vanier, the founder of the international charity L'Arche, devoted his life and talents to serving the mentally disabled, perhaps the poorest of the poor, many of whom cannot even bathe themselves or go to the bathroom without help. Volunteers spend time feeding and caring for the clients, yet they all say that these people teach them more about God and holiness than anything else! There are others, mostly unknown. When she gave a poor elderly man a blanket, she was giving warmth to Christ. Serving and caring for those who are less fortunate than us, whether they are materially poor or spiritually poor is an essential ingredient for discipleship. That is why one of the hallmarks of the Christian life and faith is serving the poor. When we serve the poor, we are serving Christ.

Every month some of our parishioners purchase food and cook a hot lunch for about one hundred men, whom they call clients, at the local Men's Rescue Mission, a 90-day alcohol and drug detox center. Besides trying to get them sober, the Rescue Mission also offers daily prayer in their chapel, GED programs, as well as a host of other job and skill training sessions. Many non-profit groups volunteer cooking meals for them, the local Boy and Girl Scouts, various sports teams, Church youth groups, and so forth. Each group also makes their own signature meal, something that only they make. Our congregation is best known for our pasta and meat sauce! When the doors open for lunch, you can see mouths water as the men wait in line for lunch. These men are hungry for pasta, but they are also hungry for hope, for a job, for deliverance from their addictions, for family connections, and for comfort and consolation. They are hungry for self-improvement. Every month we feed them pasta and sauce, but in feeding them, we are being fed and nourished.

Every month we see all kinds of men, old and young, black and white, tall and short. Judging from some of the conversations which I overhead, many did not have a full school education. Others were wearing mismatched clothing. Chemical dependency knows no age, color, creed, or gender. Yet, as we fed them plates of pasta, sauce, bread, and banana pudding, they all said, "Thank you." By serving them a simple meal of pasta, bread, salad, and pudding, we were serving the poor, we were serving Christ. Unfortunately, the lunch lines never end at the Rescue Mission. Every month there are about 100 men, some of the same faces appear, and others are new. The cycle continues every month: new faces, hungry stomachs, and hopeful attitudes. Every meal we serve, we are serving Christ.

FOOD FOR THOUGHT

1. We know from the Bible that God cares for the poor and needy. Many parishes and congregations have a food bank, clothing collection, or special financial offerings for the poor. What can you do in your parish or community to serve those who are less fortunate?

2. Pray for the poor. If you see a homeless man or woman while driving to work or while doing your errands, say a quiet prayer for them. Collect your spare change in a jar at home or work and at the end of the month donate those funds to a local charity.

3. Take some time and read about the lives of some of the people mentioned in this chapter. Try to find inspiration from their writings. Does anything in particular stand out? Is there a particular way that you can serve the poor? We are all different and can use our talents and abilities in different ways.

4. For further reading: Amos 2, Psalm 10, Psalm 72, Matthew 25.

CHAPTER FOURTEEN

JESUS THE CARPENTER

He left that place and came to His home town, and His disciples followed Him. On the sabbath He began to teach in the synagogue, and many who heard Him were astounded. They said, 'Where did this man get all this? What is this wisdom that has been given to Him? What deeds of power are being done by His hands! Is not this the carpenter, the son of Mary and brother of James and Joses and Judas and Simon, and are not His sisters here with us?' And they took offence at Him (Mark 6:1-3).

When I was growing up every year our parish community conducted a Christmas Eve service followed by a special Christmas play sponsored by the Church School children. The priest read the Christmas story in parts, some from Luke and some from Matthew. There were the usual casts of characters from Jesus' birth: Mary, the shepherds, the angels, a few sheep, the wise men, and, of course, Joseph. Because I was usually the tallest boy in my Church School class, I was usually Joseph. Being the introvert that I am, I was not overjoyed with everyone looking at me and snapping pictures, but alas, I was supposed to play Joseph.

The gospels do not provide a lot of information about Joseph. We do know that he was betrothed to Mary and that he was from the lineage of David. We also know that the angel Gabriel came to Joseph announcing that Mary would bear a child. Later, Gabriel also came to Joseph in a dream warning that Herod was planning to kill the Christ child and that they had to go to Egypt, and then a little while later, the angel told Joseph to return to Nazareth where he resided. These very limited passages are the only things that we know about Joseph. Joseph is a minor character in the Gospel story. Joseph appears very briefly in the beginning of the Gospel story and then goes offstage just as he entered: quietly.

In the ancient world, there was a very small wealthy class who were almost always the most educated and then the majority of people were form the working class, peasants, farmers, and day laborers. Some passages in the Gospel refer to Jesus as the *carpenter's son* meaning that Joseph was a carpenter. The gospels do not say specifically that Jesus was a carpenter, but most people did what their father did. If the father was a baker, the son would be a baker.

If the father was a blacksmith, the son would be a blacksmith. However, there is a small problem. The English word carpenter is actually builder or master builder in Greek, the word is *teknon*, which is very similar to the word architect, which means master builder. If Joseph was a builder, he probably was a stonemason, not a woodworker. When you travel to the Middle East and the Holy Land in particular, you will quickly see that there are few wooden structures, most of the buildings are made from type of limestone. All of the ancient buildings that have survived are made from some type of stone.

Jesus was raised in Nazareth, a small village in the middle of the Galilee area. Not too far from Nazareth was Sephoris, a large Roman city that was being constructed during Jesus' lifetime. Sephoris was large with several main roads going through it alongside with covered sidewalks. There was a public bath as well as a theater and a Jewish synagogue, which dates from the first century. Archeologists tell us that Sephoris was a major Roman city, and judging from its size, people from around the Galilee area would have traveled there for trading and shopping. If they were Jewish, they would have visited the synagogue. If they wanted to go shopping, there would have been plenty of places for that. If Joseph was a stonemason, as many peasants were manual laborers, then there is a possibility that he would have worked in or around Sephoris.

The gospels refer to Jesus as a *teknon*, master builder or architect, which echoes one of Jesus' parables about building a house on a good foundation:

> '*Everyone then who hears these words of Mine and acts on them will be like a wise man who built his house on rock. The rain fell, the floods came, and the winds blew and beat on that house, but it did not fall, because it had been founded on rock. And everyone who hears these words of Mine and does not act on them will be like a foolish man who built his house on sand. The rain fell, and the floods came, and the winds blew and beat against that house, and it fell — and great was its fall!' (Matt. 7:24–27).*

This passage also happens to be the last parable in a series of teachings and parables that are contained in the Sermon on the Mount. After three long chapters that contain teachings on prayer, forgiveness, almsgiving, discipleship, Jesus uses this parable as a final example of what it means to follow His teachings. Those of us who follow Jesus' teachings, who listen to the Word of God and fulfill the Word of God are like builders who build on a strong foundation, which is so strong that even the winds and rain will not knock it over. Jesus compares this with the fool who does not heed His words and builds his house on the sand. It may look strong at first, but eventually the sand will give way and the house will fall.

Ironically enough, my accountant repeated Jesus' words to me a few years ago. We were talking about people buying beachfront property and the high costs of it and the great return on investment. No matter where you live, everyone likes waterfront property. However, he told me all you need is one big storm or a small hurricane and you will be in trouble. He related that a long time ago, one of his clients built a dream house on the beach. He and his wife saved up a lot of money and finally bought the place. Then a big storm came; it was windy and rainy and hurricane force winds. The next morning the couple woke up and drove to their house only to see just the roof popping up and floating on the ocean, the storm completely destroyed the house. The lesson learned: buy a house in the mountains and rent at the beach, you will not go wrong! I never thought I would hear a Gospel story from an accountant but how true! Beachfront property is wonderful, and everyone loves to watch the waves come in and a beautiful sunrise or sunset on the beach, yet they are usually not ready for the high risk involved. While telling me this story, the accountant made sure to emphasize, "All you need is one storm and you're finished." All it takes is one.

A similar teaching is found in Paul's letter to the Corinthians. Here Paul tells the Corinthians that he is like a skilled master builder, building up the Body of

Christ, and he is doing this on the foundation, which is Christ. Paul says that other people who come after him are supposed to continue building on this foundation, until the entire building is built up and developed:

> *According to the grace of God given to me, like a skilled master builder I laid a foundation, and someone else is building on it. Each builder must choose with care how to build on it. For no one can lay any foundation other than the one that has been laid; that foundation is Jesus Christ. Now if anyone builds on the foundation with gold, silver, precious stones, wood, hay, straw — the work of each builder will become visible, for the Day will disclose it, because it will be revealed with fire, and the fire will test what sort of work each has done. If what has been built on the foundation survives, the builder will receive a reward. If the work is burned, the builder will suffer loss; the builder will be saved, but only as through fire (1 Cor. 3:10–17).*

> *So then you are no longer strangers and aliens, but you are citizens with the saints and also members of the household of God, built upon the foundation of the Apostles and Prophets with Christ Jesus Himself as the cornerstone. In Him the whole structure is joined together and grows into a holy temple in the Lord; in whom you also*

are built together spiritually into a dwelling place for God (Eph. 2:20–22).

As you therefore have received Christ Jesus the Lord, continue to live your lives in Him, rooted and built up in Him and established in the faith, just as you were taught, abounding in thanksgiving (Col. 2:6–7).

Even though Paul was a tent maker by trade, he speaks like he was a true construction worker. Paul is extremely worried that all his work will be in vain. He encourages the other apostles to build on the foundation which he laid, which is Christ. The building metaphor is also a mixed metaphor. At one point, Paul speaks of Christ as the foundation or the bottom part of the building. In the letter to the Ephesians, Paul speaks of Christ as the cornerstone or the headstone, which in building terms is one of the most important parts of a building. The cornerstone holds the building together. It is sometimes called the capstone. Paul wants his readers to know that building on any other foundation aside from Christ will be futile. When we build on the strong foundation of Jesus, our building will stand firm and will not be shaken.

FOOD FOR THOUGHT

1. St. Paul says that he built on a strong foundation which was Christ. Are you building on a strong foundation? Or are you building on sand and stones?

2. St. Paul devoted his life to building up the body of Christ. Everywhere he went, he encouraged and inspired people to keep living the life of faith. Try to build up others during this coming week. Even though you might not work full-time in ministry, a hug, phone call, card, or email to a friend becomes the oil of mercy for those who are suffering.

3. For further reading: 1 Corinthians 16, Ephesians 5, Philippians 4.

CHAPTER FIFTEEN

JESUS THE WANDERER

Now when Jesus saw great crowds around Him, He gave orders to go over to the other side. A scribe then approached and said, 'Teacher, I will follow You wherever You go.' And Jesus said to him, 'Foxes have holes, and birds of the air have nests; but the Son of Man has nowhere to lay His head.' Another of His disciples said to Him, 'Lord, first let me go and bury my father.' But Jesus said to Him, 'Follow Me, and let the dead bury their own dead' (Mark 8:18–22).

My family is very rare. I was raised in a small suburban town and attended local public schools and maintained the same friendships from kindergarten all the way through high school. My parents worked at the same jobs and, like me, maintained their same friendships. We attended the same parish for over twenty years. We never moved. We enjoyed social and financial stability, and we were more or less content with life. My wife was raised in a similar manner. Most of our friends and neighbors have moved multiple times and have changed jobs and career just as many times. We live in a society built around change, change, and change. We are always seeking the new and improved. Stability provides comfort, security, and a sense of belonging.

According to the gospels, we know that Jesus was born in Bethlehem and then immediately Joseph took Jesus and Mary and escaped to Egypt. Joseph took his family back to Galilee. Jesus began His preaching and teaching ministry after His baptism. From then on, Jesus was virtually homeless, depending on the goodwill of others in order to survive. Jesus, together with His disciples, traveled throughout the Galilee area preaching and teaching the good news.

Jesus traveled extensively. His home base was the villages and towns surrounding the Sea of Galilee: Capernaum, Bethsaida, and Magdala. We know that Jesus' first miracle was at Cana of Galilee, not too far from Capernaum. He also took His disciples about a two-day journey up to Caesarea Philippi where Peter confessed that Jesus was the Christ. Jesus also traveled to Jerusalem several times as well. At one point in the gospels, Jesus and His friends took a short boat trip across the Sea of Galilee to Gergasa, where Jesus healed the man possessed by demons. Jesus was very much like the itinerant preachers in 19th-century

America, circuit riders, who traveled from parishes and villages throughout the countryside, spending a few days or weeks in one area before moving on to somewhere else. They would spend several days in one area preaching and hosting ten revivals and then moving onto the next town or village. The Methodist preachers were known for this style of ministry, and even today, a Methodist pastor may stay a few years in one parish before moving on to another one.

As an itinerant preacher, Jesus traveled lightly. At one point, He even told His disciples:

> *These twelve Jesus sent out with the following instructions: 'Go nowhere among the Gentiles, and enter no town of the Samaritans, but go rather to the lost sheep of the house of Israel. As you go, proclaim the good news, "The kingdom of heaven has come near." Cure the sick, raise the dead, cleanse the lepers, cast out demons. You received without payment; give without payment. Take no gold, or silver, or copper in your belts, no bag for your journey, or two tunics, or sandals, or a staff; for laborers deserve their food. Whatever town or village you enter, find out who in it is worthy, and stay there until you leave. As you enter the house, greet it. If the house is worthy, let your peace come upon it; but if it is not worthy, let your peace return to you. If anyone will not welcome you or listen to your words, shake off*

*the dust from your feet as you leave that house
or town. Truly I tell you, it will be more tolerable
for the land of Sodom and Gomorrah on the day
of judgment than for that town (Matt. 10:5–15).*

This passage appears close to the end of the Sermon on the Mount. Jesus calls the twelve disciples whom He teaches. He sends them out two by two into the villages and areas, preparing them to continue His Kingdom building. Interestingly, Jesus does not do everything Himself; He equips His disciples to continue His own ministry. What does He tell them, do not take two tunics or gold or silver or sandals, and if the people do not listen, then wipe off the dust from your feet and keep on moving; go from village to village if needed. In other words, Jesus does not want His disciples to settle down in one place; He wants them to move around and spread the Gospel. Later, when reading the Book of Acts and the epistles, we see that the Apostle Paul continued this preaching ministry by traveling around the Roman Empire, and he too, like Jesus, traveled with ministry teams or coworkers: Silas, Timothy, John, Mark, Barnabas, and Peter. They assisted one another in the ministry, helping further the Gospel message to the ends of the earth.

In many ways, we are all fellow travelers on this earth. Our physical homes are just temporary dwellings, because our true home is in heaven with God. By virtue of our baptism, we are called to be dead to this world. Of course, we need shelter to protect us and transportation to get to work. We need money to buy things. However, the thrust of Jesus' message in the above passage is to remind us about our relationship with material possessions. Jesus does not want His disciples to get too attached to the material and physical objects.

In the early years of our marriage, we moved into our new apartment with just two car loads of items: books, clothes, CD's, a few pictures, and a few other odds and ends. Three years later, we moved from our apartment in New York to a slightly larger apartment in North Carolina. During the first three years of our marriage, we accumulated enough things for us to rent a small moving truck. After a year in our apartment, we moved to our first house, and we were thrilled. After four years in our first house, we moved yet again to a slightly bigger house, but this time we had to hire a large moving truck. Every time we moved, we had to rent a bigger and bigger moving truck. When unpacking all of those boxes, I realized how many things we accumulate that we really do not need. How many of us need to keep old papers from college or old textbooks? While cleaning out the office closet, I filled three Xerox boxes full of old papers, receipts, and things that I later shredded or threw away in the garbage.

Throughout the gospels, Jesus reminds us that our life is not about accumulating material things, but acquiring the Holy Spirit. In other words, we need to have material things to survive. I need my car to get me to work. I need this laptop computer so I can continue writing. We need clothes and shelter. However, while we have these things, we need to be reminded that there are more important things in life, such as love, mercy, forgiveness, justice, compassion, and service.

FOOD FOR THOUGHT

1. Do you have a lot of possessions? Have you thought about donating some of your possessions to charity? Do you need to keep everything?

2. Jesus tells us to build up treasures in heaven where moth and rust do not consume and where thieves cannot break in and steal. Are you storing up treasure in heaven?

3. Thinking and acting like you are just a traveler here on earth might lighten your load a bit. We often struggle trying to maintain our status, maybe even comparing our lifestyle with others. Be aware that our time on this earth is limited; make sure to make the most out of it by living a Godly life.

4. For further reading: Luke 15, Matthew 10, Mark 6:1–13.

ADDITIONAL IMAGES OF JESUS IN THE NEW TESTAMENT

1.	Alpha and Omega	Rev. 1:8, 17; 2:8; 21:6; 22:13
2.	Cornerstone	Eph. 2:20
3.	Spiritual Rock	1 Cor. 10:1; 1 Cor. 10:4
4.	Head of the Church	Eph. 1:22, 4:15, 5:23
5.	Firstborn of Creation	Col. 1:15
6.	The Amen	Rev. 3:14
7.	Lion of Judah	Rev. 5:5
8.	Morning Star	Rev. 22:16; 2:28
9.	The New Adam	1 Cor. 15:22
10.	Emmanuel	Mt. 1:23
11.	High Priest	Heb. 3:1, 4:14, 9:11
12.	Bridegroom	Mt. 2:19, 9:15, 18:23
13.	Son of Abraham	Mt. 1:1
14.	Author of Life	1 Cor. 14:33, Acts 3:15; Heb. 5:9, 12:2

15. Savior	Lk. 1:67; Jn. 4:42; 1 Jn. 4:14
16. Firstfruits	1 Cor. 15:20–3
17. Holy One of God	Mk. 1:24, Lk. 4:34, Jn. 6:69

RECOMMENDED READING

Bianchi, Enzo. *Praying the Word: An Introduction to Lectio Divina*. Kalamazoo, MI: Cistercian Publications, 1998.

Brown, Raymond E. *Christ in the Gospels of the Liturgical Year (Expanded Edition with Essays)*. Collegeville, MN: The Liturgical Press, 2008.

Martin, James. *Becoming Who You Are*. Mahwah, NJ: Hidden Spring Books, 2006.

Mills, William. *A 30 Day Retreat: A Personal Guide to Spiritual Renewal*. Mahwah, NJ: Paulist Press, 2010.

_____. *Our Father: A Prayer for Everyday Living*. Rollinsford, NH: Orthodox Research Institute, 2008.

Norris, Kathleen. *Amazing Grace: A Vocabulary of Faith*. NY: Riverhead, 1998.

Taylor, Barbara Brown. *An Altar in the World: A Geography of Faith*. New York, NY: Harper Collins, 2009.

Williams, Rowan. *Where God Happens: Discovering Christ in One Another*. Boston, MA: New Seeds, 2005.

ABOUT THE AUTHOR

Fr. William Mills, Ph.D., is the rector of the Nativity of the Holy Virgin Orthodox Church in Charlotte, North Carolina. Fr. Mills received his theological education at St. Vladimir's Seminary in Crestwood, New York, and his doctorate in Pastoral Theology from the Union Institute and University in Cincinnati, Ohio. He is the author of numerous commentaries on the Gospel readings in the liturgical year as well as two books on pastoral ministry in the Orthodox Church. For more information about Fr. Mills, visit his website at www.williamcmills.com.